personally focused and culturally relevant. We all have "miraculous potential," but so few of us ever really tap into it. In this seminal work, Wayne Chaney shows us how! This is an essential read for all those who are serious about knowing God in a greater way and fulfilling their dreams.

—*Van Moody*
Bestselling author, *The People Factor* and *The I Factor*

Every once in a while the kingdom of God releases a fresh voice with a fresh vision. Wayne Chaney is the manifestation of this truth. His book *Your Miraculous Potential* is not only an innovative examination of the Word and will of God for His children in our day, but it is presented in an articulate manner that will grip your heart and spirit with the higher, deeper, broader, wider possibilities and new dimensions of a miraculous relationship with the living God. Page after page will take you from revelation to reality as Chaney unveils scenes from his own spiritual autobiography, grounded in biblical theography, and demonstrates the potential of our progress and maturity in the will and desire of the Father. You will learn how God wants to lovingly transition you from…mere study of the miraculous—in the lives of other people and other times—to personal, practical experiences of the God who still speaks to us and desires our spiritual response and experience of the miraculous. This work will give you a hunger and thirst…for the promises of God and His prophetic power for your life's journey.

—*Kenneth C. Ulmer, PhD, DMin*
Presiding Bishop, Macedonia International Bible Fellowship

Your Miraculous Potential: though the title sounds somewhat mystical, ontological, and ethereal, the principles in this book will enhance you mentally and emotionally, as well as spiritually. It does not simply make the miraculous an unattached, outward contributor but also takes into account the psychological effect that a new God-awareness can have on us. This God-awareness embellishes both the psychological and spiritual regions of our lives so that we become more than we ever thought we could be. Here is the latch that releases the "miraculous." This significant work will bless you richly.

—*Bishop Noel Jones*
Noel Jones Ministries
Senior pastor, City of Refuge Church, Gardena, California

YOURMIRACULOUS
POTENTIAL

MAXIMIZING GOD'S GIFTS OF
CREATIVITY, GUIDANCE, AND POWER

Wayne CHANEY JR.

WHITAKER
HOUSE

Your Miraculous Potential:
Maximizing God's Gifts of Creativity, Guidance, and Power

Wayne Chaney Jr.
1535 Gundry Ave.
Long Beach, CA 90813
www.waynechaney.com
info@antiochLB.com

ISBN: 978-1-62911-695-2
eBook ISBN: 978-1-62911-696-9
Printed in the United States of America
© 2016 by Wayne Chaney Jr.

Whitaker House
1030 Hunt Valley Circle
New Kensington, PA 15068
www.whitakerhouse.com

LC record available at https://lccn.loc.gov/2016044829

1 2 3 4 5 6 7 8 9 10 11 **ᗐ** 23 22 21 20 19 18 17 16

DEDICATION

To my wife, Myesha:

You are the living embodiment of the virtuous woman in Proverbs and lovingly hold my heart captive. You have been and shall forever be "Wayne's Girl." I dedicate this book to you and our children, Wayne, Reign, and Cadence, who have already arisen to call you "blessed." You all have enriched my life in every way. Everything I do is for God's glory and to make you proud.

ACKNOWLEDGMENTS

Pastor Joe Chaney Jr. (PaPa): You taught me what love and integrity truly looked like, and you were, for me, a shelter from life's rain.

Maxine Chaney (Granny): You sacrificed so much for me to experience the best, and I will forever be in your debt because of it. I love you more than you will ever know.

Denise Johnson (Mom): You gave me life and lovingly guided me back into the arms of my heavenly Father in the years when I lost both my belief and conviction. Thank you for allowing the Lord to use you to anchor my soul. P.S. Your prenatal prayers over me have prevailed.

Wayne Chaney Sr. (Dad): Your commitment to the service of humanity and pursuit of nobility in an age of dishonor have inspired me and all who know you. Yet, it is your consistent love for me and the Chaney family that continually connects my heart to yours.

The Martins (Tom, Myra, Monique, Keisho, Kiara): You are not in-laws but family. The depth of gratitude I feel toward you all cannot be captured with words. You have given me the love of my life, defended my honor, and opened your lives and hearts to me, and for that I will forever be grateful.

The Johnsons (Bill, Caleb, Camden, Dietrich): It seems like yesterday that we all lived under the same roof, crammed into the car for road trips, and listened to Aunt B and Grandma Johnson sing Christmas carols in the key of Z flat. While life has moved our physical addresses, it has not changed the place you all have in my heart.

My Chaney Siblings (Chris, Joseph, Maya): I love you all dearly and am impressed daily with the sense of greatness that rests over you. I stand in eager anticipation for all our heavenly Father will do in you and through you in the days to come. Your miraculous destiny awaits!

My Antioch Church Family: Your love for me and relentless pursuit of Christ have been a saving grace in my lowest moments. Thank you for keeping my arms lifted and for your willingness to continually follow me into unknown territory. Never lose your hunger for His best!

My Village (family, extended family, friends, and colleagues): Your love, prayers, and contribution to my life have enriched me in every way.

Don Milam: Thank you for hearing heaven's frequency in my message and connecting me to a literary outlet that would appreciate it. You were the answer to the prayer my wife and I prayed in our room the night before we met.

Lois Puglisi: Your genius should not be credited to your literary insights alone, but is also due to your theological proficiency, diversity of experience, intuition, and passion for His kingdom. Thank you for all of your editorial excellence. It was an honor to work with you.

CONTENTS

FOREWORD

This is a significant book in that it confronts what is, in my opinion, the greatest single issue facing the church throughout the world today, namely, whether we will seek to represent the kingdom of God with the best of human ingenuity, machinations, and plans or allow God to capture us and represent Himself in His awesome power through us. The latter, God representing Himself through us, will be achieved as the church at large and every born-again member, in particular, bows to the government of God. This will, in turn, prompt the greatest awakening in world history.

Wayne Chaney, in personal passion and lifestyle, represents the title of this presentation, *Your Miraculous Potential*. This book reminded me of something I heard almost half a century ago: "If we could but show the world that being committed to Christ is no tame, humdrum, sheltered monotony but indeed the greatest adventure the human spirit could ever know, the world, standing outside our churches, would come rushing in, and we could expect the greatest revival since Pentecost"!

Moses found out the difference between what he could accomplish as a capable shepherd with an ordinary staff in his hand in managing a herd of mindless sheep—and what he could do to change history by throwing his staff on the ground at the Lord's directive and picking it up again as the staff of God. (See Exodus 4:1–5.) Before that event, there was a good man, a good staff, and a very difficult assignment involving millions of people being extracted from a life of slavery. After that event, the staff, thrown down and picked up again, became the flash point that changed history as God's people were returned to their own land.

The world is waiting for citizens of the kingdom of God who, finding their authentic identities as individuals and as a united enterprise, and accepting their destinies as the people of God, change the landscape of planet Earth by becoming living manifestations of the sons of God. Unknowingly, this is what the world is waiting for: common men and women, indwelt and empowered by the Spirit of God and reflecting the person of Jesus Christ, prepared to co-labor with God in reaping the greatest harvest of souls since the beginning of time. Reading books like *Your Miraculous Potential* will move you toward a desire to be in that number.

After finishing this book, don't just sit there! Start moving in your destiny as a twice-born, God-indwelt, Spirit-anointed child of God, throwing down the rod that identifies you as a mere human being and picking it up again as an ambassador of the eternal King and His kingdom, living amazed at what God can do as Jesus the Christ is lifted up, drawing all men to Himself.

Read this volume carefully, commit yourself to God without reservation, and begin moving in your limitless potential. Thank you, Wayne, for this clear, graphic, and vivid offering to this broken, burdened, and bothered generation.

—*Jack R. Taylor*
President, Dimensions Ministries
Melbourne, Florida

AN INVITATION

We are all wired with the sense that there is more to our existence than we experience regularly. Whatever our daily cycle, we share the same sentiment: either consciously or subconsciously, we realize we are living beneath our potential. I am not speaking about the classic sense of human potential, as in developing our gifts and abilities. Neither am I speaking in regard to issues of personal motivation, educational pursuits, or life goals. I'm talking about an internal longing that persists until it is satisfied by something greater than the ordinary. This desire is without question a craving for the fulfillment of a potential that often goes untapped.

There is more to people's fascination with fictitious superheroes than the need to be entertained, or to fantasize about escaping the limitations of their own reality. If we were completely honest with ourselves and allowed time for reflection, we would have to admit it is the ability of these superheroes to break the bounds of natural existence that intrigues us most about them. In fact, their ability not only intrigues us but also resonates with the deepest part of our being—that part of us that reaches deeper than the physiological or cerebral and into our non-material essence. The area with undiscovered capabilities, designed by the Creator of all.

Our natural conditioning often causes these abilities to be suppressed, neglected, or even denied. We are taught to distance ourselves from, or to approach with skepticism, anything inexplicable, mysterious, or experientially spiritual. However, denying these realities actually causes us to deny a most valuable part of ourselves.

Sadly, even people of faith have to be convinced of their spiritual possibilities—at times, with as much persuasion as is needed for atheists, agnostics, or general seekers. I speak before many live audiences, and as a disclaimer (usually before presenting the same subject matter contained in this book), I often have to remind people that they believe in a God they can't see, in spiritual beings they can't physically touch, and in a final destination with no empirical data attached to it. The question I pose to them is, "Why stop there?" Since you're already out on the proverbial limb according to the standards of natural logic, why not embrace in its fullness the reality you profess?

With that said, I understand that people have warranted reservations about miraculous claims due to spiritual abuses, bad theology, heretical teachers, and outright quacks. I, too, am concerned about much of what I hear in regard to this subject matter, but I refuse to throw out the baby with the bathwater. And while some people may be leery due to observed abuses, others may be cautious because of their particular theological stance, denominational bent, or long-held beliefs. If this is where you are, please know that my intention is not to argue exhaustively for the place of the miraculous here, though some defense for it will emerge later in this book. My primary focus is not to defend against the critic but rather to bring the willing participant into the reality I myself am experiencing.

I would love to see the emergence of those who could carry the miraculous with a sense of normalcy and a tremendous level of character. Those like the biblical figure Joseph, who was able to tap into knowledge beyond mere human observation but was sound of mind enough to be given the highest governmental appointment of his time.

For far too long, believers have been as partisan as narrow-minded politicians, dividing themselves into camps that suit their comfort zones, levels of exposure, and experience. In terms of political leanings within the United States, the majority of the population would be classified as either Democrat or Republican. Loyalties and ideologies exist outside of these parties but don't reflect the affiliation of the masses. I've found a unique parallel among people of faith. Though their allegiances aren't always articulated as clearly and their views don't have a universal label, they tend to fall into one of two categories, what I will call "Spirituals" and "Groundeds." "Spirituals" are usually concerned with having an experience or an encounter with God and less concerned with the theological credibility associated with the encounter. They tend to rely heavily on revelation and believe that miraculous encounters and abilities are possible and available today. "Groundeds" prefer time-tested knowledge to experiential encounters; they rarely speak of revelation they've received but rather of what they have studied in the Scriptures. Groundeds theoretically believe in the miraculous but actually feel that most of the supernatural activity of God occurred when the miraculous events described in the Bible originally played out. While very few of them will readily admit this, they have subconsciously made it their default position.

Similar to our political climate, the tensions between these two groups are very real. They even have their own unofficial labels for each another. The Spirituals brand the Groundeds as "uninspired," and the Groundeds classify the Spirituals as "mystics." I imagine that as they read the beginning pages of this book, some are attempting to determine whether my words are consistent with their particular camp of choice or "spiritual party," so they'll know whether they should continue reading. For the sake of inquiring minds, I think it is important to set the record straight: while I find strengths in both parties, I feel that their shared vulnerability is a partially blind but radical commitment to their exclusive ideologies.

Unfortunately, as in politics, when an individual desires to venture across the set boundaries, that person risks the criticism and sometimes ostracism of their own group. As for me, I choose to organize outside of the parameters of the major spiritual parties. I choose to accept the strengths of both while rejecting their areas of vulnerability. I choose to have both knowledge and zeal, biblical scholarship and revelation, structure and freedom, and insights into supernatural events of the past with fresh faith for miraculous manifestations today. My "party" could be described as those who fall into the category detailed by Jesus when He talked with the Samaritan woman at the well. I am in the camp of believers who encounter and relate to God "*in spirit and truth*" (John 4:23, 24 niv84). In context, the "*truth*" mentioned here speaks of the proper spiritual dynamics and order necessary to engage Jehovah on His terms (which the Jewish custom possessed). The "*spirit*" portion of the passage deals with the experiential encounter with the divine (which many of the Samaritans seemed to be having without the formal insights of the Jews). Jesus suggests that the Creator of all is looking for "Grounded Spirituals" or "Sound Mystics"—that's my affiliation!

While balance within the above-mentioned tension is extremely important, my goal in this book is to help us reclaim the supernatural dimension of our existence and our miraculous potential in God. You can rest in the fact that I'm biblically sound and that the accounts that follow are true, with no exaggeration for effect. My life and character can be confirmed by many seasoned spiritual leaders across the globe; but more importantly, my heart is weighed by God.

PART ONE: AWAKENING

1

SEEDS OF THE MIRACULOUS

It was a day that produced some of the most extraordinary events of my life—but it could not have begun in a more ordinary way. After getting up and following my usual morning routine, I left the house for my weekly breakfast appointment with a few fellow pastors from our beachside city in California. Arriving at our regular meeting place, the local Marriott, I made my way to the hotel's restaurant to find all three guys waiting for me. It was now the established pattern for me to be the last to arrive to the party, so naturally there were a few minutes of banter before we got into any serious conversation.

I ordered my customary Belgian waffle with eggs over easy, and then an awkward silence fell. This quiet was eventually broken by a comment from my friend David. While I can't recall his specific words, the heart of what he said still resonates with me. He mentioned the seriousness of the times we were living in and that God was orchestrating the unfolding of His will by giving us all a unique sense of acceleration in relation to our lives and ministries. This was in response to the unspoken tension we all brought to the table— we were still dealing with the unexpected and sudden deaths of three spiritual leaders in our area within a two-week period. While his comments weren't to suggest that God had somehow taken their lives in order to sharpen the focus of His people, he did imply that our experience with the loss could have that effect.

I don't know that I received David's words as definitive at that point. After all, the untimely deaths could have been used by God to accelerate His purposes, but they might also have been natural occurrences—and completely coincidental. In response, I made a quick, clever joke to lighten the mood and to escape my internal theological deliberations. We spoke about David's comment for only a few more minutes before shifting topics.

THE GROUND GAVE WAY

As our late breakfast came to a close, we paid the bill and walked out to the parking lot together. Our quartet soon became a duo—David and me—and the subject matter I had been able to cleverly escape at the breakfast table became the central topic of our discussion once more. Again, while I don't fully recall the details of our conversation, I do remember well a word that seemed to trigger a unique experience for me. When he uttered the word "judgment," I got a quick mental image of what I imagined to be the throne of God, and it felt as if the ground underneath my feet gave way, as if I were standing on a trampoline, and everything around me seemed to jolt. I quickly braced myself between two cars, and when the sensation subsided, I asked my friend, "Did you feel that?" To my surprise, he responded, "Feel what?"

Maybe it was just me. Could this have been a physiological instability as opposed to an environmental one? Although I seemed to have had an unusual experience, I restrained my alarm and allowed David to continue talking. After another twenty seconds or so of conversation, he mentioned the word "judgment" again, and to my astonishment, there was an exact reoccurrence of the first incident triggered by that single word. At this point, I stopped him and explained precisely what I was experiencing and about the word that had triggered the episodes. Being a spiritually-sensitive and discerning man, David suggested that I pray about it and seek the deeper meaning (if there was any). Still a bit shaken up, I agreed, got into my car, and drove off.

While on the road, thoughts of the recent deaths of our three pastor friends, David's comments, and that morning's unexplained incidents all pervaded my mind. Was God really up to something? Were these events just coincidental, or was there a divine connection between them? It was all too much to grasp at that moment, so I turned on the radio as a temporary distraction and headed to the coffee shop.

EMERGENCY ROOM

After getting my daily triple cafe mocha, I jumped back in the car to head to my office. But before I was able to pull out of the parking lot and into traffic, I began to feel what precedes a loss of consciousness—or what they call in the medical field a "pre-syncopal episode." My body seemed to be failing, but my mind raced with many potential scenarios concerning what was happening and what I ought to do: *Should I try to step out of the car for help, and if I do, will I collapse and be hit by incoming traffic? Is this just psychological (possibly a panic attack) or was it physiological (a stroke or a heart issue)? Was this related to my morning conversation and the recent, sudden deaths of the three pastors? Were these my last moments, and if so, who should I call?*

My wife, Myesha, immediately came to mind. Not only is she the person I would want to speak with if my life were coming to a close, but she was, at the time, also a registered nurse (less romantic but very practical). I dialed her number, and when she answered I told her what was going on and that I loved her and the kids. She asked me if I thought I could make the one-minute drive down the hill to my office or go a few feet farther to the fire station. While in retrospect it probably wasn't the wisest choice, I went to the office, and then Myesha drove me to the fire station. The paramedics took my vitals and suggested that I get to the hospital emergency room immediately. When I arrived, I was promptly taken to an examining room, where a battery of tests began. After a couple of hours, a no-nonsense physician came into my room and said that one of the tests that is used to reveal the possibility of a stroke came back higher than normal and that further tests would be necessary. Before I knew it, I was on a gurney headed for a CT Scan and an MRI.

What was going on? As if my day hadn't been disorienting enough! I was thirty-three years old and the picture of health; in fact, to prove it, I had just run a full marathon with no training just months before. How could I be here? I had started my morning, as most people do, expecting the usual routine, only to find myself laid out on a stretcher facing the reality of my own mortality. Again, thoughts raced through my head. I wondered if I had a serious condition, such as cancer, or a brain tumor that would require surgery, or an incurable illness. Would I leave the hospital at all? I pondered whether my physical challenge had any connection to those of the other pastors who had mysteriously died within two weeks of my own dilemma. Was my current experience somehow related to the image of God's throne and the shaking I had felt earlier?

LIVING BENEATH OUR POSSIBILITIES

The thought of impending death often brings more clarity about life than anything else. Though the idea is rarely discussed, I would be willing to wager that more people make resolutions at funeral services than they do on New Year's Eve. What brings sobriety in those moments isn't necessarily a fear of the unknown but a fear of the *undone*. What arrested me wasn't the idea of transitioning to be with the Lord but the question of how I had used the years on earth that I'd been given. While I was involved in countless good things, my uneasiness came when I began to consider their true spiritual weight and lasting value. I realized then that some of what I had convinced myself I was doing for God actually had a great deal of personal ambition attached to it. I thought about the things that should have been a priority for me but still remained on the back burner. Likewise, I considered the things that should have been peripheral in my life but had become primary.

I had been blinded to the eternal by the immediate, and while I wanted to present my life's work before God someday, I didn't want it to be *that* day. While, by most standards, I had accomplished a great deal both spiritually and professionally, I also realized that for much of my adulthood, I'd lived beneath the possibilities. I wanted the opportunity to recalibrate the trajectory of my life. So, I silently cried out to God from my gurney, *If You will allow me to leave this hospital, I'll begin to live with more intentionality....* Then I followed up with words that opened an encounter with God that is still unfolding for me: *Please do not allow me to live beneath the possibilities in You!*

The heavens didn't part, nor did angels descend, but somehow I knew that God had honored my heart's cry. Though I didn't feel 100 percent physically, the doctors cleared me, and my wife drove me home. She scolded me (mildly) for working too hard and insisted that I take a few days off to rest. After all I had been through, it didn't take much convincing for me to agree. I responded with a feeble "Okay" and jumped into bed as soon as I got home. For the next few days, I didn't leave the bedroom, and I didn't watch any TV. I wasn't deliberately trying to be pious, but I had no appetite for trivial things. During my brief sabbatical, I read anything and everything I could get my hands on for spiritual inspiration. Aside from the Bible, I read books, articles, and excerpts from revivalists, reformers, and revolutionary spiritual leaders. One of the random articles I came across was entitled "Seeds of Revival."

The article described the legacy and observations of Frank Bartleman, one of the men who chronicled much of what took place during the Azusa Street Revival of 1906. I was captivated by a portion of the article that read, "Many today...are foolishly pursuing the effects of revival at the expense of neglecting the conditions of revival."[1] I translated the comment in this way: "People want the effects of the supernatural (or miraculous) without planting the seeds for the miraculous." At that moment, I felt a need to renew my hospital gurney prayer, so I again asked God never to let me live beneath the possibilities in Him. I wanted more than an ordinary existence, one beyond the realm of what was possible with my own ingenuity, and this was my opportunity to plant the seeds for it. In the days that followed, I made the same request, and after a time, I felt that something shifted in my spiritual life.

Many people assume that supernatural events present themselves in a spontaneous, unsolicited, and overwhelming manner. Yet for me, the majority of such experiences have emerged from humble beginnings. And God's answer to my continual prayer during the week following my hospital incident was no different. While I was in this posture of spiritual hunger, my wife happened to read aloud a biblical passage that grabbed my attention and consumed me. It was a Scripture from the book of Joel in which God called His people to cry out to Him on behalf of a land and a people who had drifted from His spiritual blueprint for their lives, dishonoring Him in the process. The message was that if they remained obstinate, He would allow the land to experience lack and devastation. However, if they would simply repent and cry out to Him, He might "*relent*" and also "*leave behind a blessing*" (Joel 2:14). Upon hearing this, I realized that this passage, written more

---

1. See http://www.theoldtimegospel.org/studies/serm13.html.

than twenty-five hundred years ago, has parallels to our own time. The mandate and urgency that seemed to grip this biblical prophet had somehow leaped through the portals of time and landed squarely on me. Let me be clear, my view of the God of heaven is not glimpsed through the lenses of an ever-present threat of disaster. However, I know that the prayers, obedience, and reverence of God's people toward Him can yield unique benefits and blessings, and prevent needless calamity.

The next day happened to be Sunday, and while I already had a message prepared, I was too enraptured by the previous night's experience to stick to our usual agenda. So, without any introduction, I stood spontaneously in the service and began to read the same passage from Joel, which was completely unrelated to anything else that had been said or done that day. To my surprise, a great reverence and an un-coached, electric, worshipful atmosphere fell over the meeting. At that moment, the *still small voice* of God (1 Kings 19:12 NKJV, KJV)—which will be demystified for us later—prompted me to call for daily fasting and nightly prayer meetings. But what happened in the days that followed exceeded all of our expectations.

2

A TASTE OF HEAVEN

Our first weekday evening prayer meeting began with a sense of anticipation, but also with a reasonable amount of anxiety for me as a leader. The people present didn't know what would happen but expected an unusually powerful experience, and all I had at the time was an instruction I believed was from God and my obedient response to it. There was no agenda other than to pray and intercede for the West Coast of the United States, which we felt was our specific assignment, the same way in the book of Joel the people of Judah had been instructed to cry out to God for their land. We prayed that God would arouse people from their spiritual slumber and cover our coast and its people as we turned toward Him. To our amazement, we believe that He not only heard our prayers but also "left behind a blessing," as promised in Joel.

"MORE OF YOU, GOD!"

One simple request we made, among others, was that He would allow us to experience more of Him. We were after more of His presence and power, and in the days that followed, there was no doubt that He honored that request. A couple of nights into our time of fasting and prayer, I stood on the platform at church and began to encourage the people to ask for more of God, and it seemed like the more we asked, the more our desire grew. However, of everyone present that night, I appeared to be affected in the most profound manner. My voice was lifted in concert with the others in attendance, and I felt my request being granted as my lips projected the one desire of my heart: "More!" Suddenly, it was as if the air in the room became heavy, a sense of God's nearness became evident, and a slight fear of what could happen if I dared request any more of His presence came over me. After a temporary paralysis due to my uncertainty, I did it. I asked for an even greater measure of His presence.

Everyone there seemed to recognize the obvious shift in the dynamics of the room. It was spiritually charged unlike any gathering we had ever held. Some people wept aloud, while others worshipped more intensely, but all were soberly aware of the fact that God was overwhelmingly present. Words are not adequate to describe my personal experience that night. I've given much thought to it; however, my most valiant efforts still fall short. Please excuse the metaphor, but it was as if an already drunk man decided to consume one last drink for the road. However, imagine that the glass is a pitcher, and that he consumed it in seconds. Since you're already conceptualizing, go on to visualize the condition of that same man in the moments following, and you'll get a snapshot of my experience. The only difference is that I wasn't drinking an alcoholic beverage but was instead experiencing more of God than I ever had before.

The experience became so overpowering that I staggered with lifted hands and tear-filled eyes and eventually fell to the floor under the waves of God's increasing presence and goodness. As I lay leveled and awestruck on the church platform, the congregation and the music seemed to grow more and more distant, while the presence of the Lord became more prominent. I felt a communion with my heavenly Father that was purer than any other experience I've ever had. If it had been possible, I would have stayed in that place forever. It was there that I got a temporary taste of the eternal contentment of heaven and what will make living forever with our Creator so satisfying. It was also there that I received a snapshot of what our prayer meetings would begin to look like from that point forward. The Lord showed me that I was only the first to experience the weight of His glory in this manner, and that as we continued to seek Him, He would visit the entire house in a similar way—and did He ever!

NOT YOUR "USUAL SUSPECTS"

What happened during the nights that followed was inexplicable apart from God's supernatural power. As promised, people in the crowd had experiences that paralleled and even exceeded my own. More supernatural events occurred than can be recalled. There were spiritual, physical, and relational miracles every night, but what made these meetings unique was that many of the people affected weren't your "usual suspects." They wouldn't have been considered "mystical," radically spiritual, or even inclined to the more experiential encounters with God; they would have fallen into the "Groundeds" category rather than the "Spirituals" group.

For example, by her own admission, Ms. White would have labeled herself a "theologically conservative secessionist," one who believed that many of the gifts of the Spirit had ceased in the first century AD. She had been a student of the Bible most of her life. She had an undergraduate degree from Biola University and had even served as an adjunct professor at Azusa Pacific University. Needless to say, she was no novice theologically.

Ms. White enjoyed the environment of our prayer meetings but rarely involved herself with us corporately. She would sit in the building's foyer, behind the glass, where she would peer in to observe our activity. Then, one night, I called for everyone present to come inside the sanctuary so that we could all be in one room. To her surprise, when she got about five steps into the sanctuary, the same overwhelming power that had hit me the first night hit her. She fell to the floor and was down for a significant amount of time (as were many others that night); and to her further astonishment, when she gathered herself to stand, she began to speak in a heavenly language, or what the Bible calls *"tongues."* (See, for example, Mark 16:17.) She was experiencing what she had taught against and what she hadn't believed in just moments before.

That night, two Southern Baptist missionaries were also present at the prayer meeting. The power of God hit them in the same manner that it had Ms. White, except that when they rose to their feet, they began to prophesy words that were beyond their knowledge. They had never functioned in that capacity before. It was as if the power and the presence of God were tangible to them. The experience was so profound that when one of them stood up the next Sunday (just a few days later) to recount what had happened, God's power filled the room and the individual again fell to the floor under that power.

In this environment, not only was miraculous power present, but physical healings also became commonplace. Clara Carpenter, the eighty-two-year-old grandmother of member Jeremy Anderson, had been diagnosed with terminal pancreatic cancer and given three months to live. We lifted up a prayer for her around the time of these meetings, and when her doctors went back in to assess her condition, there was no cancer to be found.

Ronelle, a local nurse, was dealing with symptoms that were eventually identified as leukemia. However, while participating in the prayer meetings, she began to hear the healing testimonies of others, and she believed for her own healing. She went back to the hospital in town, which was also her place of employment, and asked them to run the tests again. To everyone's amazement, her tests came back normal—as those of a completely healthy individual.

My own aunt, Joanne Davis, came into one of the prayer meetings with an extremely heavy heart and a defeated countenance. She had been forced by her doctor to cut short her vacation due to the negative results of some tests she had undergone before leaving Los Angeles for a trip to Houston, Texas. The physician called my aunt to tell her she had one of the worst cases of cirrhosis of the liver he had ever seen and that she also had blood clots all around her pancreas. Aunt Joanne returned to LA, but before going to her appointment (scheduled for the day after her arrival) she stopped by our evening session.

She did not publicly share her crisis but began to cry out to God within the atmosphere of that gathering. When it was over, she left without any sense of physical transformation or signs of change; but the next night she returned with a radically different appearance. There was no sense of heaviness or discouragement about her—only a gleeful, almost childlike, worry-free expression. Before I was able to inquire about her sudden change in countenance, she told me exactly what had happened. She had gone to her doctor's appointment that day, and after the medical staff had run tests on her for several hours, she received an apology from her doctor. When she asked, "What do you mean, Doc?" her physician responded, "We must have mixed up your charts with someone else's, because your liver is completely healthy, and there aren't any blood clots, either."

While this news excited her, she insisted that the doctor look into the charts again. Upon more careful observation, he realized that the first set of charts were indeed hers. In complete bewilderment, he simultaneously gripped his head and dropped his jaw, then exclaimed, "I don't get it!" My aunt responded, "I do," and shared with him her faith and the source of her healing, before leaving his office rejoicing.

After Aunt Joanne shared this story with us at the prayer meeting, her testimony spread like wildfire throughout the church and the community. In fact, I invited her to share her story on my weekly radio show, which is broadcast on Stevie Wonder's Los Angeles-based station, KJLH 102.3FM. A few days after that program aired, she went to the hair salon and walked into the middle of a very interesting conversation between two of her hairstylist's other clients. The women were discussing whether or not the accounts they had heard on the radio and the testimonies being proclaimed by the church were authentic. (You may be deliberating about this in a similar way right now.) One woman argued for the believability of what was being reported, based on my character as a leader. She made comments such as, "He doesn't seem like the type of person who would lie," and "He has a good reputation." The other woman said, "I like his ministry and his messages, but these claims have gone too far; they can't be true."

My aunt Joanne is not known to hold her tongue when something needs addressing. However, every time she got to her boiling point and prepared to interrupt the criticisms, her stylist would gently kick her in the back of the leg to discreetly shush her. After a while, the other women began to settle on the improbability of it all, and it was then that Aunt Joanne couldn't take it anymore and joined the conversation in an unequivocal manner. In her slightly sassy, Southern accent, she interjected, "It's real, and my nephew is real and is telling the truth!" She went on to tell them about the power of God and how she herself was one of many people who had experienced His supernatural touch.

LIVING IN THE MIRACULOUS

Since the focus of this book isn't on miracles or healings in and of themselves but rather on unlocking our fullest potential in God, I won't go into detail about the additional miraculous events—the tumors that disappeared before surgeries or the healings of loved ones that occurred the moment people crossed the threshold of their family members' hospital rooms. And if our prayer meetings were the primary focus of this book, I would not merely tell of the countless physical healings but also of the miracles of relational restoration. I can think of three couples off the top of my head who experienced the same knee-buckling power of God that I experienced early on. They, too, fell to the floor, and when they got back up, they repented of their offenses against one another, of their desire for divorce, and, in one case, of infidelity (on the part of both spouses). These couples have gone on to have some of the healthiest relationships in our ministry. Our prayer meetings were not just "confession fests" but became supernatural restoration sessions where there was confession but also instant reconciliation.

Beyond all of the spiritual, physical, and relational miracles, the harvest of people who walked down the aisle to connect with Christ and our local church was exponential. We went from having an average of ten people a week walk down our aisles to connect with Christ or our church, to fifty-plus for months, with no changes to our regular Sunday presentation. And many of those who responded to our Sunday appeals never even knew about the weekday prayer gatherings but experienced the overflow of power that spilled into our weekend services. To keep up with the ministry demand, we had to schedule additional services.

As in the first-century church, "*everyone kept feeling a sense of awe*" (Acts 2:43 NASB). There was no doubt in anyone's mind that we were experiencing something that was beyond us all. For the first time in their lives, many people felt the satisfaction of no longer "living beneath the possibilities in God." I had received the answer to my hospital-gurney prayer, and God didn't limit the experience to me but allowed hundreds of others to taste the morsels of heaven's atmosphere, as well. He allowed miraculous possibilities to become miraculous realities!

THE INTERNAL ARCHITECTURE THAT LEADS TO THE MIRACULOUS

As I reflect on the events that changed the trajectories of our lives, you would think that my attention would be placed squarely on the supernatural happenings or results that emerged from our season of prayer. However, what fascinates me is not just the external manifestation of all these wonderful events but *the internal architecture that brought them about*. The fruits are not my only pursuit. I want to be fully aware of the root system that produces such fruits. I felt—and continue to feel—like Moses, who wasn't satisfied with the benefits provided by God but wanted to know the God of the benefits. You sense the depth of Moses's desire to familiarize himself with more than blessings, miracles, and external manifestations when you read how he cried out to God, *"Teach me your ways so I may know you..."* (Exodus 33:13).

The atmosphere of our prayer meetings was only the tip of the iceberg. It served as a sign, revealing that the miraculous life is not experienced only in this type of environment but is much broader in its scope. It is beneficial for all of our endeavors; it is realized in both the overtly spiritual arenas and the seemingly practical areas of life.

My purpose for recounting the supernatural events that took place in the life of our ministry wasn't simply to cause you to marvel but rather to begin to unpack the "mechanics," or process, that preceded the miraculous. Everything we experienced during that period of time followed a simple response to a word from the Lord.

The essence of fulfilling our miraculous potential (not living beneath our true possibilities in God) is rooted in the ability to hear or discern the voice of God and then to exercise the faith necessary to respond to His divine utterances. Great books on the supernatural are plentiful, and there are a number of wonderful works that are focused exclusively on miracles, healings, and revivals. However, in many of them, these two basic principles are somehow left out. Again, hearing the voice of the Lord and responding to it in faith are beneficial not only for experiencing the kinds of miraculous events cited above but also for receiving unusual results in every arena of life. The chapters that follow were written to lead the willing soul into understanding God's ways and heaven's system for breaking the bonds of human limitation.

3

ORDINARY INSTRUMENTS

MIRACULOUS RESULTS AND MOTIVATING FORCES

Uncontrollable forest fires ignite from a seemingly insignificant spark; avalanches crash downward with the slightest slippage of rock or ice; the giant sequoia sprouts from a seed the size of a baby's fingernail—and significant movements of God are released through a divine utterance detected and responded to by those who are attuned to His voice and motivated by a desire to obey.

God uses everyday individuals like you and me, but the release of our miraculous potential begins with a passion to know Him and His ways and to clearly hear His voice. When we chase miraculous results merely for the sake of the miraculous results, it becomes very easy for us to miss God's intent for our lives. A dear friend of mine once pointed out, "Heresy is not always wrong doctrine, but wrong emphasis." Both the miraculous results and the motivating force behind them are significant. The following statement by Jesus from the seventh chapter of Matthew's gospel brings clarity and authority to this point:

> *Not everyone who says to Me, "Lord, Lord," will enter the*
> *kingdom of heaven, but he who does the will of My Father*
> *who is in heaven will enter. Many will say to Me on that day,*
> *"Lord, Lord, did we not prophesy in Your name, and in Your*
> *name cast out demons, and in Your name perform many mir-*
> *acles?" And then I will declare to them, "I never knew you;*
> *depart from Me, you who practice lawlessness."*
>
> (Matthew 7:21–23 NASB)

This passage paints a picture of individuals who were able to accomplish supernatural manifestations in the form of prophecies, deliverance, and many other unspecified miracles. Yet Jesus doesn't celebrate these fruitful manifestations; instead, He indicts those who produced them. On the other hand, the Bible is filled with specific accounts of miraculous events performed by God through human beings that *are* celebrated by Him. What is the distinction? Again, this passage indicates that while the supernatural works performed were fruitful, they weren't celebrated by God. Jesus actually called these works *"lawlessness,"* primarily because He *"never knew"* those who performed them. This statement indicates that their works, though miraculous in nature, weren't birthed out of intimate fellowship with the Lord but were, quite possibly, motivated by personal ambition or other vain pursuits. The main issue in this text is that the works were not prompted from the close relational connectivity that exists when Jesus "knows" someone. Jesus' indictment above doesn't imply that He lacked cognitive knowledge of them; instead, it speaks of the absence of intimate acquaintance with them—and vice versa. For that reason, their works, while good in themselves, were unauthorized.

The works God ultimately rewards are the ones that He Himself has authored, ones that have been done in response to a word or a directive He has given. They are acceptable to Him because they are aligned with His character and purposes. That is why releasing our miraculous potential has to do not only with the supernatural results but also with the origin and motivations of those works.

Some time ago, I came to the realization that heaven is not impressed with supernatural events or miracles that occur in or through the lives of human beings—only people bound by the confines of the natural world are impressed with these manifestations. Why? Because the essence of heaven *supersedes natural law and limitation.* There is nothing unusual about the supernatural within the context of God's divine abode; it is the ordinary atmosphere of heaven. But it becomes significant to us when that sweet essence of heaven breaks into the lives of mere mortals, adorning the world as we know it. So the life-altering, paradigm-shifting encounters people experience are not what God Himself is impressed with. After all, the power, the display, and the results are all from Him. His motivation for imparting them is love, and they give Him pleasure and satisfaction, but why should He be impressed with us for something He made possible?

What heaven does take note of and celebrate are matters such as the following, which are epitomized by certain biblical characters: our intimacy with God (Enoch), our righteous faith in God (Abraham), our desire to know the God of the miracles and not just receive the miracles alone (Moses), the reverential condition of our heart (David), and human activity that is not independent of Him but rather is continuously prompted and inspired by Him (exemplified fully by Jesus). (See, for example, Genesis 5:22–24; 15:1–6; Exodus 33:12–23; Psalm 51; John 14:10.)

If we commit ourselves to cultivating the ability to discern the voice of God and to developing the faith to humbly obey it, we will not only experience miraculous results in every area of life, but will also participate in those realities in a way that is pleasing to God. When our actions are birthed from heavenly instruction and guidance, then they are the fruit of proper origin and correct motivation—and they will yield eternal results.

ACCESSIBLE TO ALL

In light of this truth, note the depth of this statement by Jesus, who authoritatively declared, *"Man shall not live on bread alone, but on every word that comes from the mouth of God"* (Matthew 4:4). God's speaking and our response are the source and sustenance of our spiritual existence, as well as the keys that unlock our miraculous potential. For most people who are living beneath this potential, the barrier is either an ignorance concerning the voice of God, an inability to discern it, or a lack of the faith necessary to respond to what He desires.

When you cultivate the ability to hear God's voice and to respond willingly to it, you will possess insight beyond the sum of your learning; it will make you wiser than the aged and bring you into opportunities you were previously unqualified to stand in. As the psalmist wrote,

> *Oh, how I love your law! I meditate on it all day long. Your commands are always with me and make me wiser than my enemies. I have more insight than all my teachers, for I meditate on your statutes. I have more understanding than the elders, for I obey your precepts.*   (Psalm 119:97–100)

This passage from Psalm 119 has helped to define my life. I believe its truths apply not only to the wisdom and guidance I receive from God's Word but also to the wisdom and guidance I receive directly from His Holy Spirit, who gives us the heart of the Author and specific direction for the nuanced issues of our lives. (I will discuss this point in greater detail in later chapters.) If it had not been for my knowledge of the simple yet divine principles of hearing God and responding to what He says, the most fruitful experiences of my life would, for the most part, have been nonexistent. Again, these principles don't belong to me alone; they are accessible to all who desire to act on them and to bear their fruit. I am dumfounded by how many people—particularly people of faith—attempt to live spiritual lives while either rejecting or being ignorant of this most crucial dynamic. You can therefore understand why it is such a passion of mine to bring others into the life that has brought so much fulfillment to me.

Those who have known me for any length of time have been able to witness firsthand many of the spiritual fruits produced as a result of what has now become a way of life for me. Not only has living this principle yielded healings, revivals, and relational miracles (as previously cited), but also the creation of companies; the launching of a faith-based radio broadcast on a top-rated secular FM station; events that have drawn tens of thousands annually; a co-starring role on a network television show with record-breaking viewership numbers; and audiences with some of the world's most influential leaders, including sitting U.S. presidents. Not to mention the receipt of awards, recognitions, and appointments to special committees and leadership positions that were beyond my own ability or qualifications. To my recollection, every significant door that has opened in my life was first preceded by my response to an utterance from heaven.

I believe what makes these results so noteworthy is that there is not much unique or special about me in the natural sense. This is in no way or by any means a stretch of the imagination or false humility—it is fact. My ordinariness makes it extremely difficult for me to drift into a sense of personal significance apart from my relationship with God through Christ and divine inspiration. However, I feel that this is by design. God chooses *the foolish things of the world to confound the wise*" (1 Corinthians 1:27 KJV), primarily by giving them insights and wisdom through His Word or counsel that surpass all of their learning or empirical observations. He "upgrades" His servants by giving them access to His very mind in the form of revelation—both written and spoken.

In the second chapter of 1 Corinthians, the apostle Paul made this point abundantly clear when he said,

> *We do, however, speak a message of wisdom among the mature, but not the wisdom of this age or of the rulers of this age, who are coming to nothing. No, we declare God's wisdom, a mystery that has been hidden and that God destined for our glory before time began. None of the rulers of this age understood it, for if they had, they would not have crucified the Lord of glory. However, as it is written, "What no eye has seen, what no ear has heard, and what no human mind has conceived"—the things God has prepared for those who love him—these are the things God has revealed to us by his Spirit. The Spirit searches all things, even the deep things of God. For who knows a person's thoughts except their own spirit within them? In the same way no one knows the thoughts of God except the Spirit of God. What we have received is not the spirit of the world, but the Spirit who is from God, so that we may understand what God has freely given us.*   (1 Corinthians 2:6–12)

While this passage in its entirety has enough depth to fill the volumes of a small library, let us focus on the last few verses. Verses 10 through 12 reveal the unique access to the mind of God granted to us by the Holy Spirit, who resides in every believer. Verses 10 and 11 declare that *"the Spirit searches all things,"* including the *"deep things," "thoughts,"* and mind of God. The passage goes on to explain that the Spirit we've received not only searches the mind of God but also reveals God's thoughts to our minds (at His discretion). Verse 12 says, *"We have received…the Spirit who is from God, so that we may understand what God has freely given us."*

In other words, we are capable of knowing things that are beyond human knowledge—things that are in the mind of God and revealed only by His Spirit. Reading verses 10–12 together in continuity, there can be no other interpretation than this. Paul reveals that the Holy Spirit searches the mind of God in the same way our own spirits have the ability to search our minds. However, the Spirit not only searches God's mind but also shares some of God's thoughts with us mere mortals! The very idea of this should both humble us and bring us a unique sense of privilege (along with responsibility).

When we respond to words from God that are beyond our knowledge, we participate in experiences and events that are beyond our ability. The directives, revelations, and insights that come out of our communion with the Father are the sparks of miraculous genius that release astonishing results on earth. And when people who don't know the Father witness the manifestation of these results through ordinary individuals, it often causes them to seek the Source of the works, ultimately bringing glory to God.

For many believers, who are already in relationship with the Source, the manifestations create a desire to know more about the internal spiritual dynamics that produced these results—as they did for me after I experienced miraculous results in my own life and in the life of our church. I believe, as do others, that it was this same desire that drove the disciples to ask Jesus, *"Teach us to pray"* (Luke 11:1). In Jesus' life, the disciples had witnessed the external display of supernatural healings and miracles, as well as the exercise of unusual authority, powerful teaching, and divine wisdom, and they wanted to understand and emulate the spiritual relationship with God that produced them. In the chapters that follow, we will look more deeply into Jesus' life as a pattern for our own.

God's supernatural work through us, therefore, has a threefold result: it blesses the recipient(s) of the work, it brings glory to

God, and it ultimately creates in people a desire to commune with the Lord on a deeper level. I love how, in His divine wisdom, God always maximizes the efficiency of His works!

SUPERNATURALLY NATURAL

As with most things, a spiritual balance is necessary as we learn to hear and obey God's voice. I remember giving a ride to a new believer named Darrell following one of the miraculous nightly meetings at our church. After we had ridden for a little while with neither of us saying anything, he broke the silence by asking, "Pastor Wayne, when you're quiet, what are you thinking?" Similar to what we discussed above, at the heart of his question was an attempt to discover something of the internal, spiritual architecture of my life. After having observed such a powerful atmosphere and supernatural outpouring, and having established that it was from God, Darrell wanted to know how I had learned to navigate that space. He wanted to know what made me tick.

At that time, those who were participating in the evening prayer meetings were fasting daily from sunup until after the meetings concluded. So, right at that moment, I was actually thinking about food! Realizing the seriousness of his question and the depth of his desire for God, I pulled the car to the side of the road, placed my hands on his shoulders, looked him squarely in the eyes, and in the holiest voice I could conjure, responded, "Macaroni and cheese." We both laughed and then entered into more casual conversation. However, I did have an intentional lesson for him through our brief moment of levity. Many people assume that in order to live the supernatural life and release our miraculous potential, we must constantly ponder the deep things of God. But that isn't really the case, and quite honestly, it would be a bit draining to try to sustain such intense ponderings over a long period of time. Not only would it take a toll on those whom God is using, but it would also strain their human interactions, as other people tried to find points of basic human relationship and communication with ones so profoundly spiritual.

Instead, we can learn to be "supernaturally natural." The main thing is to keep your ear continually tuned to God, remain sensitive to His leading, and respond as He speaks. If we learn to stay receptive to Him and commit to becoming students of His ways, He will whisper things to us in secret that will alter the affairs of humanity.

4

THE MIRACULOUS ONE

JESUS' INTERNAL "DRIVER"

I have emphasized that the release of our miraculous potential depends on our ability to hear and respond when God speaks, and I feel it is important to validate that claim by observing these practices in the life of the most miraculously-oriented individual ever to walk the earth: Jesus Christ. He is by far the Standard—the ultimate Miraculous One. This reality is evidenced by, among other things: the numerous scriptural prophesies that were fulfilled in and through His life, which were written hundreds of years before His arrival on earth; the divine events surrounding His early life; the miracles He performed during His ministry; His authoritative proclamations; His power over sinful influences and temptation; and His glorious resurrection following His sacrificial death on the cross. In my estimation, there is no better way to grasp our miraculous potential than through His example.

This dynamic of hearing and responding to God was not only present in Jesus' ministry, but it was also the engine that drove all of His behavioral patterns. In the previous chapter, I talked about

Darrell, the new believer who was curious about my inner spiritual formation based on the external supernatural display he witnessed. As we have seen, Moses had a similar spiritual curiosity and longing. This desire touched the heart of God and caused Him to reveal to Moses things that others weren't privy to. Moses said to the Lord, *"Teach me your ways so I may know you…"* (Exodus 33:13). He wasn't satisfied with a front-row seat to the show but wanted to peer behind the curtain of the Lord's majesty in order to know Him more intimately. We should likewise be so captivated by the life of Jesus that, as His disciples did, we give ourselves not only to the study of the visible display of His miraculous life but also to an exploration of the internal "driver" that produced it.

I once attended a lecture at Oxford's Keble College, hosted by The King's University, where the lecturer, Dr. Kenneth C. Ulmer, challenged the participants to do a character study of Jesus; we were to attempt to discover how much of His life and ministry He demonstrated in His divinity, how much He carried out in His humanity, and how much He performed in His anointed humanity. Here are a few of my observations. In His divinity, Jesus said, *"Before Abraham was, I Am"* (John 8:58 NKJV), received worship (see, for example, Matthew 14:33), and allowed Thomas to address Him as *"my Lord and my God"* (John 20:28). In His humanity, Jesus ate, drank, and slept. However, Jesus performed a good portion of His ministry in His anointed humanity.

It was in this anointed humanity that, empowered by His Father, Jesus defied many of the limitations of the natural man. And it was in this anointed humanity that He became a model for us to follow in exercising our miraculous potential. A study of Jesus' internal driver is therefore significant not only because of the insights it gives us into His makeup but also because it sets a pattern by which we are able to follow Him into a dimension of life that defies our previous limitations. This model gives us a snapshot of the possibilities for us, because not only did Jesus experience deep intimacy with His Father and perform extraordinary acts, but He also led others, including His disciples, into the same reality. And not only did those who were directly connected to Him experience a miraculous existence, but so did those who received from those who were connected to Him, without ever having been directly touched by His earthly ministry.

This "more abundant," miraculous life (see John 10:10 NKJV, KJV) was meant to be experienced by followers of Jesus in an unbroken chain throughout human history and into perpetuity. Jesus did not model an anointed humanity simply for us to marvel at it but primarily to give us a sense of our own possibilities, as well as to provide us with insights into how they could become a reality in our lives. Matthew 14:25–29 captures the essence of this truth in a way that goes undetected by many Bible readers. The passage covers the account of Peter walking on water and the events that transpired just before he experienced this miraculous reality:

> *Shortly before dawn Jesus went out to them* [the disciples in the boat], *walking on the lake. When the disciples saw him walking on the lake, they were terrified. "It's a ghost," they said, and cried out in fear. But Jesus immediately said to them: "Take courage! It is I. Don't be afraid." "Lord, if it's you," Peter replied, "tell me to come to you on the water." "Come," he said. Then Peter got down out of the boat, walked on the water and came toward Jesus.*

Interestingly, Jesus supernaturally approaches the boat, walking on the water across the lake, but He does not board the vessel. Instead, He stops near it to have a conversation with the fearful disciples. Why did He stop? If His goal was merely to reveal Himself as the Messiah, receive the devotion and reverence of His followers, and cause them to marvel, His mission would be complete if He simply climbed aboard after demonstrating His miraculous water-walk. However, He stands in proximity to the boat to engage in dialogue.

I believe He did this to see whether the disciples would catch the true intent of His divine pause. None of them seem to get it except the disciple who was known to speak up for the often silent majority—the one who was also known to tap into revelation before the other eleven. It was none other than Peter. At some point in the interaction, Peter realizes that the reason Jesus demonstrated His ability to walk on water but then stopped short of getting into the boat wasn't simply for him to marvel at the feat but to imitate it. It was an unspoken invitation to the disciples to walk in what they had just witnessed. With this understanding, Peter declares, *"Lord, if it's you, tell me to come to you on the water."* To this fitting request, Jesus replies, *"Come,"* and Peter is able to join Jesus as a fellow water-walker.

I believe that Christ still gives an open invitation to every believer to follow Him into a dimension of life that is possible only with His empowerment. Like Peter, many believers today have refused to settle for living a life beneath their miraculous possibilities and have begun to request that He do the same things He performed in previous times—things they have read about in biblical accounts and in the recorded testimonies of Christ's followers through the centuries.

RESPONDING TO THE COMMUNICATIONS OF THE FATHER

The gospel of John gives us the clearest, most unobstructed view into the internal engine that drove all of Jesus' actions. Jesus allowed us to see behind the scenes of His relationship with God when He stated, in several places, that He did not act on His own accord but in response to the will or directives of His Father:

*Therefore Jesus answered and was saying to them, "Truly, truly, I say to you, the Son can do nothing of Himself, unless it is **something He sees the Father doing;** for whatever the Father does, these things the Son also does in like manner."*

(John 5:19 NASB)

*I can do nothing on My own initiative. **As I hear,** I judge; and My judgment is just, because I do not seek My own will, but **the will of Him who sent Me.*** (John 5:30 NASB)

*For I have come down from heaven, not to do My own will, but **the will of Him who sent Me.*** (John 6:38 NASB)

*So Jesus said, "When you lift up the Son of Man, then you will know that I am He, and I do nothing on My own initiative, but **I speak these things as the Father taught Me.** And He who sent Me is with Me; He has not left Me alone, for I always do the things that **are pleasing to Him."***

(John 8:28–29 NASB)

*For I did not speak on My own initiative, but **the Father Himself who sent Me has given Me a commandment as to what to say and what to speak.** I know that His commandment is eternal life; therefore the things I speak, **I speak just as the Father has told Me.*** (John 12:49–50 NASB)

*Do you not believe that I am in the Father, and the Father is in Me? The words that I say to you **I do not speak on My own initiative, but the Father abiding in Me does His works.***

(John 14:10 NASB)

These words cascaded from the mouth of Jesus, and after reading them, it becomes very clear that He not only modeled a miraculous existence but also cited the driving force of every word, deed, miracle, and revelation as being a communication from His Father in heaven. His surrendered, obedient response to those heavenly communications released the miraculous plans of heaven onto the earth through Him. This being the case, it is baffling to me that we are often taught to mirror the behavioral patterns of Jesus without giving much consideration to the engine that drove those behaviors. Most seminaries and other religious educational institutions, created to train those who instruct the masses in spiritual matters, don't even offer a course or a seminar on this principle that was central to the life of Jesus. It is no wonder, then, that something so vital to our spiritual journey is so foreign to many. It is this omission in our spiritual instruction that causes many to miss the critical link to an abundantly fulfilling existence.

Various words and phrases from the above passages in John, such as *"sees," "hear," "will of Him," "taught,"* and *"told,"* all refer to communications or directives given by the Father to Jesus. God works in a similar way in our lives. In the Bible, references to people receiving visions and revelations, being led by God, and so forth are synonymous with God speaking. All of these terms and others deal with the guidance of God in the lives of His people, but for the purpose of this book, I will summarize them simply as the ability to hear God.

GOD'S DIRECT GUIDANCE AND THE SCRIPTURES

In later chapters, I will discuss in more detail the relationship between the Bible and our hearing from God directly and personally today. However, I feel it's important that we briefly address this issue now. The Bible gives us the objective Word of God, or the big picture. It reveals God's nature and the nature of human beings, God's general instructions for humanity, insights into spiritual realities, and examples of thousands of years of interactions between the heavenly Father and His children. While the Bible gives God's broad direction, it is the work of the Holy Spirit to apply God's general, objective will to our specific, subjective lives and circumstances.

As we observe Jesus modeling for us the lifestyle of anointed humanity, we don't get the sense that He simply rolled out the biblical scrolls (Torah) whenever He wanted to be guided by God. Instead, we see an Individual who knew the Scriptures thoroughly but also apparently communed with God personally—a Man who not only read the Book but also conversed with its Author. In contrast, Jesus revealed a huge failing in the spiritual walk of the religious leaders of His day when He declared to them,

> And the Father who sent me has himself testified concerning me. You have **never heard his voice** nor seen his form, **nor does his word dwell in you**, for you do not believe the one he sent. You study the Scriptures diligently because you think that in them you have eternal life. These are the very Scriptures that testify about me, yet you refuse to come to me to have life.
>
> (John 5:37–40)

Jesus accused the most scripturally literate sect of His time of never having heard the voice of God and of not having His Word dwelling in them! Interestingly, at the time of this indictment by Jesus, the Pharisees were a group of religious leaders who personally committed more Scripture to memory (individually and collectively) than any other group on earth. Jesus showed, in essence, that it is quite possible for us to know Scripture yet not allow God to lead us into His purposes. We can therefore see the necessity not only of knowing Scripture but also of being guided by God through the person of the Holy Spirit, who still directs and speaks to willing participants today.

I believe God intentionally leaves us with certain "blind spots" in relation to the Bible in order to keep us from becoming modern-day Pharisees. I am convinced that the God of all creation, might, and majesty wants us to relate to Him personally and will never limit every encounter with Him to the study of His Book. The Bible is intended to be navigated for us by His Spirit, who was given to nudge us into personal communion and relational intimacy with its Author.

One of the reasons, through the Scriptures, God captured thousands of years of His speaking with His people was that He wanted to show us what was consistent with His will. In general, if there is ever any personal revelation, guidance, direction, or word we feel "led" to follow that seems to violate what He has previously said in His Word, we should immediately reject it as an option for us. Again, the personal guidance of God does not contradict the written Word of God but always complements it. Yet His relational guidance through the indwelling Holy Spirit covers some areas of direction for our lives that are not specifically addressed in the Bible.

For example, for a man who is considering marriage, the Bible provides the general attributes of what he should look for in a virtuous woman, but the Holy Spirit can help him in making a decision about whether or not he should marry a particular young woman he is interested in. Similarly, the Bible speaks of the necessity of hard work but doesn't specifically indicate which job we should take. The Holy Spirit can help us to narrow the possibilities between, for example, a job offer in Austin, Texas, and one in Chicago and can redirect us even when we've chosen inaccurately.

Consider this illustration. My last few cars have come equipped with a feature that I can hardly function without now; it's called "Blind Spot Assist." For the most part, when I am driving, I depend on the three mirrors—the rearview mirror and the two side mirrors—that are standard in most vehicles. They give me a good view of my surroundings, helping to keep me safe from collision on the crazy roads of Southern California. However, there are some portions of the road that the mirrors can't cover. At certain times, such as when I prepare to shift lanes, my observation through those mirrors is insufficient; in those moments my Blind Spot Assist kicks in and warns me, as needed, of adjacent cars that are dangerously close. A triangular "red alert" symbol appears in one of the side-view mirrors; this alert is not a mirror but is, rather, a complementary aid that indicates what the mirror doesn't.

Spiritual people must begin to understand that God is not simply a "mirror" or even a "blind spot assist" but an entire "guidance system" and therefore reserves the right to utilize all of the equipment in His arsenal to enhance our encounters with Him and the world around us. This is why He will speak to us in a variety of ways through His Word (the Bible) and by His Spirit.

The reason I've taken time here to briefly address this issue is not to defend against the skeptic but to promote rest rather than anxiety in the hearts of all who desire to live the life God intends by releasing their miraculous potential. Various ways in which God speaks will be covered more specifically in later chapters. However, my purpose here has been to reveal and expand our understanding of the essence of the miraculous life and to adopt as our motivation for behavior the same dynamic that motivated Jesus.

When we hear the voice of the Lord speak to us in the present, and cultivate the faith to respond to His communications with confidence, it will unlock our miraculous possibilities. Again, this reality is not reserved for a select few but is available for all believers. For far too long, we've left what Christ intended for His entire body to only a small number of believers whom we have labeled "spiritual." It is God's desire for all of His people to hear from Him, to respond to His voice, and to witness the unfolding of what is beyond their ability, for His glory.

OUR UNTAPPED SPIRITUAL CAPACITY

Every year, I teach the content of this book to live audiences in various cities in order to experience the joy of seeing everyday people brought into this reality. A few years ago, after teaching one group about the various ways God speaks and about our need to respond in faith, I felt led to move from merely teaching information to the participants to encouraging true spiritual formation in them. So I stopped my presentation for a moment and asked each member of the audience to pair up with someone by joining hands. While some of the people knew those in proximity to them, many ended up being paired with a complete stranger. One such individual was my mother, who had come to the meeting for a bit of inspiration. She had wrestled with depression for years and was having an extremely pronounced bout of it the week of that meeting. In addition, she was being haunted by the idea that she was going to die young. It didn't help that her mother had died at age sixty-two and that she felt she wouldn't make it even that long. This same fear had come and gone for much of her life, but it was unusually heavy on her mind and heart that week.

Without revealing anything of her struggle to Ursula, the woman sitting next to her, she simply grabbed the woman's hands and waited for further instructions. I asked each person to silently look into the eyes of the person whose hands they were holding and ask God to speak to them about their partner. After a couple of minutes, I told them to simply share what they felt God had shared with them, without overly worrying about making an error, since this was practice hearing from God in a safe learning environment. Within seconds, the room erupted into a glorious commotion. I saw irrepressible smiles, tears, eureka-like expressions, and embracing, and I heard laughter, shouts of joy, and deep cries of relief from many who had been delivered from oppressive pain.

I learned what had produced many of these expressions as we gave those who had received significant words or insights the opportunity to share. While there were more testimonies than I can recount, one stood out to me above all the others—not because it was the most captivating, significant, or glorious but simply because of my relationship to the one who gave it. Usually, the closer your relationship to a person who has experienced a truly miraculous encounter, the greater the impact on you because it comes with tremendous credibility. You have the joy of hearing the testimony, made even greater by knowing the previous journey of the testifier. For the same reason, we celebrate every young person who graduates from college but are brought to tears when attending the graduation of a loved one. And so, I was especially moved by the testimony of my mother, who took the platform to explain why tears flowed down her face like a mountain creek.

She first shared her history of depression and how she had wrestled all week with thoughts of an early death. She then went on to describe the communication her partner had shared with her in the Spirit-led activity. Ursula had received a simple image that had no profound significance to her personally. Not only had she viewed it as uninspiring, but she also felt it to be so ordinary that she almost didn't share it. What she saw was this: a fleeting image of my mother in old age with a full head of gray hair. The Spirit-breathed thought or utterance from God that Ursula had almost dismissed was the pebble that began the avalanche of healing in the life of my mother that is still felt to this day.

Who could have predicted that a simple exercise would erupt into countless supernatural encounters? God had brought encouragement and healing by revealing things related to the meeting participants that were beyond empirical observation. At this gathering, no celebrated prophets, global personalities, or professional Christian musicians were in attendance—just "ordinary" people who learned how to hear God's voice and respond to it by faith. Those present that day hadn't simply stumbled into a chance encounter with the power of God but had discovered the driving force of Christ, the most Miraculous One planet Earth has ever seen!

Now that we have established a good foundation and working definition for our miraculous potential, we need to move from description to personal discovery. Again, the goal isn't to simply add more to our knowledge base but to unlatch the door to our untapped capacity. But first, if at the heart of our miraculous potential is the ability to recognize and respond to the divine utterances of God, then the fine-tuning of our spiritual hearing is essential.

PART TWO: HEARING

5

THE HEART AND HEARING

SOMETHING VALUABLE TO TEACH US

In those days the word of the LORD was rare; there were not many visions.   (1 Samuel 3:1)

This may seem like an unusual verse to begin a chapter on hearing the voice of God. However, when the Bible records the scarcity of *"the word of the LORD,"* it is worthwhile to take note of people like Samuel who had the ability to hear from Him. Those individuals have something especially valuable to teach us. The lessons learned in lean times are only magnified when His words are plentiful. So the book of 1 Samuel is the perfect place to begin a chapter on discerning the voice of the Lord. If the prophet Samuel could hear God in his time, when *"the word of the LORD was rare,"* we can most certainly expect to hear from God in our own time.

Samuel's day was a time much like ours: there was a tremendous amount of religious activity, spiritual leaders spoke on behalf of the God of heaven, people worshipped corporately, offerings were collected, and most people within Israel lived functional lives. Working, socializing, going to market, and observing one's religion were the order of the day. The only problem was that God rarely spoke to the corporate culture or even to individuals. Yes, the people did have the written law of Moses—the first five books of the Bible—but they seldom received any specific guidance from the God of heaven.

This was the setting in which God spoke to a young man named Samuel, who steadily gained a reputation as a prophet whose words were attested and reliable. The Scriptures say, *"The LORD was with Samuel as he grew up, and he let none of Samuel's words fall to the ground"* (1 Samuel 3:19). Samuel was somehow able to hear God with clarity at a time when very few people could detect heaven's frequency. We can take a lesson in discerning the Lord's voice from the account of his early life. Again, if Samuel was able to hear God during a period when there was a revelation famine, then we should be able to find clues in his life that will allow us to hear from God during any period of time and in the midst of any cultural condition.

WHY WAS GOD'S WORD RARE IN ISRAEL?

Before we discuss these clues, we should understand why heaven was essentially silent at that particular time in Israel. Sometimes God allows periods of healthy silence in our lives to create within us a spiritual appetite or hunger for more of Him and His Word. However, that wasn't the case during the long spiritual void in the days of Samuel. It had to do with the hearts of those who were the nation's spiritual leaders.

According to the law of Moses, the priests were allotted specific portions of the meat of sacrificed animals, after the fat was cut off to be burned as holy to the Lord. The meat that remained after the priests took their portions was also considered part of the sacrifice. (See Deuteronomy 18:3; Leviticus 7:31–34.) Sometime before Samuel was born, a practice developed in which, after the fat was cut off and the meat was boiling, the priest (or his servant) would take a three-pronged hook, plunge it into a pot of boiling meat, and keep whatever he could bring up with the hook. This practice in itself appears to be a deviation from the specific instructions in Scripture. But the sons of Eli, the high priest and judge of Israel, took it even further. As priests serving under their father, they went directly to the people who were offering their sacrifices and demanded some of their meat raw, before the fat was even cut off, setting an ungodly example and violating God's commandment. If anyone protested that the fat should be cut off first to be burned to the Lord, he was told that if he didn't hand over the meat, it would be taken from him by force.

Not only did Eli allow his sons to dishonor God and His people in relation to these sacrifices, but he also did not stop them from other corrupt behavior, such as sleeping with the women who were assigned to serve at the doors of the temple. The sons' problem apparently started with their inability to control their physical appetites and expanded to an inability to temper their sexual appetites. (See 1 Samuel 2:12–17, 22–25.)

Allow me to briefly digress here to speak about the biblical discipline of fasting. The reason fasting is such a significant spiritual practice is because there is often an inextricable connection between our various appetites. If one appetite is ungoverned or out of control, it's only a matter of time before the others will be affected. However, when we master one of our appetites, it often makes it easier to gain mastery over the others. My friend Ray Jones shares the same principle in a way I've come to appreciate, saying, "When I have the ability to give up something I have a right to [food], it makes it easier to refrain from something I don't have a right to [unhealthy sexual appetite]."

In Samuel's day, the time had come for the Lord to fulfill His promise to remove Eli and his sons from the priesthood because of the family's wickedness. (See 2 Samuel 2:27–36; 3:11–14.) God had rejected them because Eli had done little more than "talk tough" to his sons; he had failed to make them cease their detestable behavior or to remove them when they refused to do so. Often, spiritual climates and their potential are hindered not only by what leaders do personally but also by what they allow to be done on their watch. You can be a righteous pastor, parent, or business owner, but if you turn a blind eye to rebellion or offensive behavior in your church, your home, or your business, the spiritual atmosphere will eventually be significantly hindered.

As 1 Samuel 3:1 indicates, the atmosphere of the priesthood and the hearts of the priests were so polluted on Eli's watch that God decided to limit His communication in the form of words and visions. However, although the word of the Lord was rare during that period, it wasn't long before the Lord began to speak to Samuel, who represented a new righteous priesthood.

Two contrasting categories of people are depicted in the second and third chapters of 1 Samuel: (1) those who couldn't hear the voice of God due to their rebellion and violation of God's previous instruction; (2) someone who was able to hear the heavenly utterance so clearly that he thought a human being was calling out to him from nearby! In the next chapter, we will observe God's initial interaction with Samuel to gain insights into how God speaks and how we can hear Him. But let's first examine the lives of Eli and his sons more closely so we can better understand what hinders the clear reception of God's voice in our lives.

HINDRANCES TO HEARING GOD'S VOICE

The Bible emphasizes that Samuel was righteous from childhood. While hearing God's voice doesn't require perfection (in that case, who would qualify?), Samuel's righteousness is meant to be contrasted with the wickedness of Eli's sons, who not only engaged in wrongdoing but were internally unaligned to God and His purposes for His people. This unfortunate reality is evidenced in their ability to treat holy things as less than common through their manipulation of God's people, God's sacrifices, and God's plan for sexuality. Not much has changed today. In any context, a clear sign that spiritual decline is at an all-time high is when spiritual leaders don't respect their own authority and platform, people's resources are being manipulated or misappropriated, and the morally weak become sexual prey for those whose care they are entrusted to (usually in that order). This was the case in relation to Eli's sons, but long before their spiritual decline became so pronounced, I'm sure they allowed the guidance (voice) of the Lord to be hindered in their lives. Let's look at two ways in which this occurred.

REBELLION AND MISALIGNMENT

One of the hindrances to hearing God's voice that we see represented in Eli's sons is rebellion, unrighteousness, sin, or spiritual misalignment; Eli's sons were aware of their unrighteous actions but did nothing to change them. Such things usually cause us to miss the clear and compelling communication and guidance of the Lord. Now, before you begin to disqualify yourself, thinking that you can't hear God's voice because of sins you've committed or failures you've had, it's important for you to understand a couple of things. First, as my friend Anthony Walton once articulated, "God knows the difference between frailty and rebelliousness," and He doesn't deal with people's frailty in the same way He does their insurrection. To the one whose heart's desire is to please God and do His will, an abundance of grace is present to aid in the effort and to forgive sins and failure. As long as you're alive and have a desire for God, you can move from misalignment to alignment with Him.

The Scriptures say, "*The mind governed by the flesh* [sinful nature] *is hostile to God*" (Romans 8:7); it rarely embraces His words, even if He does speak. It is not that God stops speaking when we are engaged in unrighteousness; rather, it is a matter of *how* and *what* He speaks when we are no longer aligned to His will for our lives. When we are outside of His will, He rarely speaks words of guidance. His speaking at these moments comes in the form of admonition as opposed to revelation. He creates a righteous discomfort within us in order to move us back into His will, where we can receive revelation again. And remember, revelation is utterance from God that becomes the spark that releases the miraculous, bringing fresh guidance, direction, insights, peace, joy, and more!

In Romans, the apostle Paul showed us that if we want to receive clearer heavenly communications and know the will of God, we must disconnect from the "*pattern of this world*" (unrenewed and ungodly thoughts, actions, and behavioral patterns) and renew our minds: "*Do not conform to the pattern of this world, but be transformed by the renewing of your mind. Then you will be able to test and approve what God's will is—his good, pleasing and perfect will*" (Romans 12:2). Notice that the byproduct of a renewed mind is the ability to "*test and approve what God's will is—his good, pleasing and perfect will.*"

When we disconnect from unrighteousness and connect to the desires of God as revealed in His Word, through the power of His Spirit, it will help tune our spiritual ears to His voice. It is in this position that we can more accurately recognize and identify the will of God. It increases our ability to be in harmony with heaven's frequency and to be receptive to it. (Knowing this, it is no wonder the voice of the Lord was so hampered before the arrival of Samuel!)

Another cause of misalignment/disconnection from God's will is a lack of balance in relation to the entirety of His truth. Again,

biblical imbalance or heresy is not always wrong doctrine; sometimes it can be an incorrect emphasis on good doctrine. When we
overemphasize any biblical truth to the neglect of other biblical
truths or handle it out of proper context, problems will emerge. For
example, the church today has become consumed with emphasizing
the mercy of God to the point that we often fail to mention the need
to live in His righteous will for our lives. God's mercy is a pillar of
the faith and something I preach on and talk about regularly. I need
the mercy of the Father and couldn't live a day without it. But while
the mercy of God covers our sins, receiving His mercy is not a guar-
antee that we will be receptive to Him or be "fit for the Master's use."
(See 2 Timothy 2:21.) The balance is this: God's mercy in salvation
covers our sins, while our righteous living, in the power of the Holy
Spirit, postures us to hear and discern God's will more accurately.

Therefore, we can be saved but living well beneath the miraculous possibilities available to us due to a lack of righteousness
in our lives. Once we become aligned with His will, our spiritual
abilities will be heightened. You may be thinking, *I can name various individuals who habitually dishonor God, His people, and their
ministry by their unrighteous actions and habits, but they still appear
to receive supernatural insights or results.* There are various reasons
why this may be the case, but one thing is clear: while such people
may produce results, they will always fall short of what would have
been possible through their lives if they'd been truly aligned with
God and His purposes.

When I was in high school, I ran track for one of the premier
secondary school track programs in the country. While I was good,
I was certainly not the best athlete on our team. Our school produced more professional athletes than any other in our country's
history and was voted *Sports Illustrated*'s School of the Century.
Needless to say, the competition there was extremely stiff. While
there are athletes from my school who have gone on to become

household names, ironically, you've probably never heard of those who were the most talented. One student in particular was the best natural athlete I've ever personally known. Yet he never followed the recommended dietary plan, was rarely seen working out in the weight room, seldom stretched, and was even known to smoke significantly before big meets. On one such occasion, he left a smoking session in one of the bathrooms and went out to win his event in one of the largest meets of the year. The entire team marveled at how he could shun all of the disciplines and preparations that most of us lived by and still perform at that level. However, his ability to do that never fascinated me. What consumed me was the thought of unseized opportunity.

I write about my friend from my high school track team because I want to emphasize that we not focus on the wrong thing. There are those who seem to get results while throwing to the wind the lifestyle that produces heightened outcomes, but the sad reality is that they will always live beneath their divine potential. Sure, this athlete won the school's largest meet without any preparation, but he never became an Olympian, which was completely within the realm of possibility for him. This book isn't for those who are satisfied with partial results; it's for those who (like me) pray that God will never allow them to fall beneath their promise. My goal is to help build spiritual Olympians, not mere local legends!

Let's look, specifically, at how unrighteousness, misalignment with God, and rebellion against Him lead to an inability to hear from Him. First, when God wants to speak to us or desires to give us an encounter with Him, but we desire to hold on to unrighteousness, our guilty conscience often causes us to run away from intimacy with Him—instead of embracing it. The same thing happened to Adam and Eve in the garden of Eden after they disobeyed God; they ran and hid from the voice of the One with whom they had once communed. Willful unrighteousness robs us of our closeness to God and His best counsel, which emerges through our intimate encounters with Him.

As I mentioned earlier, when we're outside of God's will, His words to us are rarely about the plans He has for us in the future but usually concern our current lack of alignment with Him. At these moments, we mainly have a sense of conviction rather than a spirit open to conversation with Him. When people are in this state, they often attempt to suppress, avoid, or discount the communication from God that convicts them of the unrighteous behavior they don't want to give up. At some point, this rejection of God's prompting can repress His voice of correction. Ironically, what escapes our minds in such moments is that the God whom we are pushing away is the same God we need for continued direction and insight for our lives! We forget that the God of the correction we don't want is also the God of the revelation we need.

Therefore, to shut out God's voice in one area where we don't want to hear from Him also shuts it off in other areas where we do want to hear from Him. When we harden our hearts to avoid His correction, we will likely become too calloused to receive His revelation. Rarely does God speak around our rebellion to get us back to business as usual.

I remember applying to and being accepted by one of the more academically rigorous theological schools in the country. I attended the orientation with a great deal of excitement, but my zeal for the institution was short-lived when I realized that it seemed to be void of spiritual life and that the teaching bordered on what some would call heresy! However, because of its reputation and the program's compatibility with my schedule, I decided to stay.

After more time elapsed, I began to feel the Lord leading me to depart, but instead I justified my presence there. Now the leading of the Lord became conviction, followed by feelings of grief; but because of my professional goals, I again suppressed the prompting of God. I remained there, even though I was now somewhat grieved at an institution I desired to attend. The downside of suppressing God's direction was that I needed to hear from Him for the weekly sermons I had to prepare and give to our church, as well as for professional projects and for daily insights and guidance for my family. I needed the Holy Spirit to illuminate the words of Scripture for me and to give me guidance every day. Like the scenario I outlined above, when I rejected the guidance of God in the area I didn't want to budge from, I also short-circuited His direction in other areas where I needed to hear from Him the most. My ministry, personal life, and inspiration suffered tremendously during that season of my life. I lacked clarity, focus, fresh revelation, and the miraculous favor I had become accustomed to.

I somehow expected to turn off the switch of heavenly utterances during the day and then switch it back on in the evening. This might be possible to some extent and for a period of time, due to God's mercy, but He has a way of picking up where He left off—rather than where you want Him to be when "switched" back on. When I sought His divine insights for business concerns, civic affairs, church planning, and family matters, my mind would only be filled with thoughts about the point of my departure from His will. Eventually, the heaviness I felt and my desire to be restored to harmonious spiritual intimacy with God led me to leave that particular institution. The restoration of unique guidance, unusual peace, and overwhelming favor that followed was inexplicable apart from His miraculous working in my life. I hope this illustration reveals how powerful it can be to abandon unrighteousness and realign with God's will. Not only does it have the ability to bring these results, but it also unlocks a greater capacity to hear God's voice.

WRONG HEART POSITION OR MOTIVATION

A second hindrance to hearing the voice of God is misplaced motivation or an unwholesome heart position toward Him. As we compare Samuel with the sons of Eli, we see the difference between a heart that was pure and devoted to God and hearts that were corrupted.

A couple of years ago, my then eight-year-old son was riding in the car with me after one of his school's chapel services, and he couldn't wait to share what he had learned, exclaiming, "Daddy, God can do anything!" Wanting to stretch his philosophical mind, I paused briefly and then responded with a resounding, "No, He can't!" If my son's jaw had not been attached to His face, it would have fallen to the floor. It was as if shock, confusion, disgust, and terror hit him at the same time. Uncomfortable seeing him in that condition, I went on to relieve his tension by explaining some things God cannot do. I shared, "He cannot lie, He cannot fail, He cannot break a promise." I concluded the series of "cannot's" with, "He cannot view us without seeing the conditions of our hearts."

There is no way that God can see someone's pretense without the underlying reality, their veneer without their core, or their actions without their true motivations. The words of Hebrews 4:12–13 help to illustrate this point, but I rarely, if ever, hear this passage taught in its full context.

> For the word of God is living and active and sharper than any two-edged sword, and piercing as far as the division of soul and spirit, of both joints and marrow, and able to judge the thoughts and intentions of the heart. And there is no creature hidden from His sight, but all things are open and laid bare to the eyes of Him with whom we have to do.
>
> (Hebrews 4:12–13 NASB)

When we read this passage, we usually equate the word "*sword*" with the Bible, or the written Word of God; we rarely consider the writer's expansion of the idea. But by the time we come to verse thirteen, this sword doesn't seem to be a book but rather a Person.

With phrases like *"no creature hidden from His sight"* and *"all things are open and laid bare to the eyes of Him,"* it is crystal clear to me that this passage is not simply about our getting into the Word (Bible) but rather about how the Word (the living Christ) gets into us with His piercing gaze.

Further, the Greek word for *"sword"* here is not a battle sword but rather a *machaira,* a short sword or dagger, such as one that was used by the priests to inspect the internal integrity of an animal sacrifice before it was presented. Christ's view of us is so comprehensive that it can distinguish between the nuances of our souls and spirits and the thoughts and intentions of our hearts.

God has very little tolerance for external displays that lack internal sincerity or authenticity. This is the reason Jesus was hardest on the religious leaders of His day—their emphasis was external, to the neglect of their internal heart positions. (See, for example, Matthew 23:27.) It is also why Ananias and his wife, Sapphira, both appear to receive an unwarranted judgment for a "white lie" (see Acts 5:1–11), while David is touted as a "man after God's own heart" (see 1 Samuel 13:14; Acts 13:22), even though he had indefensible atrocities on his record. Ananias and his wife allowed evil intentions to control their hearts while pretending to perform an act of charity. Conversely, having a heart that was open and dedicated to God was what allowed David to receive his label, even though he later committed adultery, conspiracy, and murder. As the Lord told Samuel, *"Man looks at the outward appearance, but the* Lord *looks at the heart"* (1 Samuel 16:7 niv84).

Having the right heart posture is the prerequisite to properly engaging with God. The position of our heart is a vital component of our encounters with the Lord; depending on its state, it can enhance or hinder our ability to hear Him. Jesus made an interesting connection between the heart and hearing and understanding God's Word when He declared,

In their [the crowd's] case the prophecy of Isaiah is being fulfilled, which says, "You will keep on hearing, but will not understand; you will keep on seeing, but will not perceive; for the heart of this people has become dull, with their ears they scarcely hear, and they have closed their eyes, otherwise they would see with their eyes, hear with their ears, and understand with their heart and return, and I would heal them."

(Matthew 13:14–15 NASB)

In this passage, Jesus connects the people's inability to hear or to perceive spiritual matters not to the quality of their intellect, zeal, or external customs, but rather to their heart position. In fact, He indicates that their spiritual blindness, deafness, and dullness are all rooted in their poverty of heart, or deepest internal motivation. I believe that a similar internal bankruptcy is what caused Eli and his sons to stop perceiving the voice of God, and it is what eventually caused God to cease speaking to them altogether.

Take a moment now to position yourself to receive all that God has for you as you continue in this journey toward your miraculous potential. Let Him know how much you desire to be a Samuel in your generation and not a son of Eli. Begin to release any unhealthy attachments; acknowledge to Him where you are weak, and ask for His help! Cry out to God, as David did, for *"a clean heart"* and *"a right spirit"* (Psalm 51:10 KJV). He will hear and answer!

6

POSTURE AND PRIME TIME

SILENCE BROKEN

We have seen that the days of Eli the high priest were a time of spiritual decline in Israel in which hearing a word from the Lord or receiving a vision from Him was rare. We've also explored the reasons why Eli and his sons forfeited their ability to obtain revelation from the Lord. In 1 Samuel 3, we find a description of how the long period of virtual silence from heaven was broken. In place of Eli, God desired someone new to lead the nation, both spiritually and judicially, to whom He could entrust His words. He wanted someone whose heart was sensitive toward Him, someone who would not only hear His voice but also respond to His instructions by faith.

At that time, God sent out His word, and it found Samuel, a vessel through whom He could release His miraculous guidance and power. And it is from the following passage of Scripture that we will develop a working foundation for hearing the Lord. We will begin to see those clues in Samuel's life that will allow us, too, to receive from God.

The boy Samuel ministered before the LORD under Eli. In those days the word of the LORD was rare; there were not many visions. One night Eli, whose eyes were becoming so weak that he could barely see, was lying down in his usual place. The lamp of God had not yet gone out, and Samuel was lying down in the house of the LORD, where the ark of God was. Then the LORD called Samuel. Samuel answered, "Here I am." And he ran to Eli and said, "Here I am; you called me." But Eli said, "I did not call; go back and lie down." So he went and lay down. Again the LORD called, "Samuel!" And Samuel got up and went to Eli and said, "Here I am; you called me." "My son," Eli said, "I did not call; go back and lie down." Now Samuel did not yet know the LORD: the word of the LORD had not yet been revealed to him. A third time the LORD called, "Samuel!" And Samuel got up and went to Eli and said, "Here I am; you called me." Then Eli realized that the LORD was calling the boy. So Eli told Samuel, "Go and lie down, and if he calls you, say, 'Speak, LORD, for your servant is listening.'" So Samuel went and lay down in his place. The LORD came and stood there, calling as at the other times, "Samuel! Samuel!" Then Samuel said, "Speak, for your servant is listening."
(1 Samuel 3:1–10)

THE POSTURE FOR RECEIVING

While God reserves the right to speak to any person at any time, there are certain realities that will increase the frequency with which He communicates with us, as well as amplify the intensity and heighten the experience. We can actually posture ourselves for these benefits.

The boy Samuel ministered before the LORD.
(1 Samuel 3:1)

We can't get beyond the first verse of the above passage without being presented with one of its primary insights: Samuel *ministered* before the Lord. His ministering to the Lord under the supervision of Eli meant that he carried out some of the practical duties in God's house; the concept also includes the idea of the praise and worship of God.

I could write an entire book on the topic of worship alone, but for the sake of conciseness, I'll borrow a description from the *International Standard Bible Encyclopedia*, which defines worship as "honor, reverence, homage, in thought, feeling, or act, paid to men, angels, or other 'spiritual' beings, and figuratively to other entities, ideas, powers or qualities, but specifically and supremely to Deity."[2] It indicates the worshipper's response or reaction to recognizing the worth of the one receiving the worship. One of the most common acts in worship is to bow in humility at the thought of the object of that worship or (more specifically) in the presence of the one being worshipped. This posture of bowing or yielding can be either literal, figurative, or both. It can be expressed using one's body or by yielding one's will to one who is greater.

Again, we could discuss endless insights on the topic of worship, but for our purposes, we will narrow its scope to the following four points, which describe its place in enabling us to hear God.

1. Worship focuses both our minds and spirits on the Lord. It tunes us to His frequency because it is an act that engages both of these aspects of our nature and directs them toward Him. In the natural world, if you want to hear from someone, you acknowledge that person and give them your full attention. Worship generally helps us to accomplish this in relation to God.

2. Worship magnifies, or glorifies, the Lord, which the Bible exhorts every believer to do. (See, for example, Psalm 34:3.) When the Bible instructs us to magnify the Lord, it is not that our

---

2. See http://www.internationalstandardbible.com/W/worship.html.

"magnifying" Him makes God any greater than He already is. It simply means that as we honor Him, verbalize His greatness, and reflect on His divine characteristics and deeds, our own view of Him changes. He actually becomes larger and more prominent in our own minds and hearts. When this happens, our doubts, fears, limitations, and distractions begin to subside. If we learn to magnify the Lord, it will minimize the things that cloud the spiritual communication airways.

3. Similarly, true worship always elevates the perspective of the worshippers and brings them closer to the perspective of God. Spiritual pilgrims in Israel traveled annually to the temple in Jerusalem, which was situated at the top of a mountain; as they did so, they would sing "psalms of ascent." The idea was that with every word they sang, they were one step higher and closer to the temple (the abode of their Lord). Today, when we worship, we don't physically ascend, but we do spiritually ascend, and as we do, we draw nearer to a fresh encounter with the Lord, the Ruler of all. Like a mountain that is broad at the base and narrow at the top, with every intentional word of sincere devotion that we offer the Lord, we narrow the focus of our scope until He alone is in our sights. It's in that place that He speaks to us words in concentrated form that are potent enough to shift our reality.

4. This next point is a spiritual mystery, but the Bible declares that God "inhabits the praises" of His people (see Psalm 22:3 KJV) or is *enthroned upon* [their] *praises* (NASB). Many people ask me the difference between praise and worship, and I usually respond, "The difference between the two can't be explained by definition but must be experienced through encounter." I can employ the same dynamics in either praise or worship, but I know when the spiritual atmosphere has shifted into one of worship because, while I continue to lavish my love on God, the encounter begins to have a profound effect on me. My will now becomes malleable for Him

to shape, and my heart becomes fertile ground for the seed of His utterance. There is a bowing of the body, the will, or both.

When Psalm 22 speaks of God "inhabiting" the praises of His people, it does not refer to His *omnipresence* (His being everywhere at once) but to the fullness of His presence. It was His prominent presence that the psalmist spoke of as the manifestation that was *"enthroned upon"* the people's praises and created a shift in the corporate or personal atmosphere of a given worship environment. Even though New Testament believers possess the indwelling presence of God's Spirit, a significant manifestation or filling of the Spirit still occurs when God's people praise Him and begin to enter into worship. There is a sense of divine communion, and things begin to bow and submit to the Lord of our hearts—whether physical bodies, limited perspectives, hardened hearts, or brittle wills.

Always remember that those who posture themselves as worshippers position themselves to hear from God!

THE PRIME TIME FOR RECEIVING

The term *prime time* often evokes thoughts of the most popular television shows—programs that command the viewership of millions and can launch the careers of unknown actors, making them household names. It also speaks of the peak time in the broadcast schedule for the maximum return on advertising dollars.

While lots of people would desire any spot on network television, prime time is the period many people in the entertainment business vie for. While it can take as much effort to create a TV program that will air during a fringe time slot, such a show will usually yield significantly fewer benefits than one aired during prime time. This reality makes those few precious hours of prime time the most coveted of the day in television broadcasting.

Is there a comparable "prime time" for clearly receiving heavenly guidance or other communications from the Lord? While we know that God can speak at any hour of the day or in any circumstance to any person, are there periods of peak encounter or maximum spiritual yield? I believe there is an interesting clue tucked away in 1 Samuel that answers these questions in a way that is consistent with the tenor of Scripture; it says that *"the lamp of God had not yet gone out"* (1 Samuel 3:3). This often-overlooked line not only helps us to visualize the scene of Samuel's encounter with God, but it also gives us insight into the hour in which God approached Samuel, and it identifies the time in which the events that followed unfolded.

The priests in the tabernacle or temple would light the lamp in the evening, and the wick would burn out by early morning or before dawn. Could the early morning therefore be prime time for those who seek divine guidance or heavenly utterances? Again, while I acknowledge that God can speak to us at any hour of the day, I do believe there are time periods, particularly in the early morning, in which we can have heightened spiritual sensitivity and receptivity. Like television prime time, these peak hours yield greater results for the same effort that would bear lesser returns at another time.

By exploring several brief passages of Scripture, we can find this reality confirmed in the lives of others in the Bible who walked with the Lord:

+ Before Samuel was born, his own mother, Hannah, who at that time was barren, got up early to worship the Lord after being blessed by the high priest. Then Hannah and her husband returned home, and she soon received her promised son.

  Then they arose early in the morning and worshipped before the LORD, and returned again to their house in Ramah. And

> *Elkanah had relations with Hannah his wife, and the* LORD
> *remembered her. It came about in due time, after Hannah*
> *had conceived, that she gave birth to a son; and she named him*
> *Samuel, saying, "Because I have asked him of the* LORD.*"*
>
> (1 Samuel 1:19–20 NASB)

♦ In the wilderness of Judah, David cried out to God, *"O God, You are my God; early will I seek You; my soul thirsts for You; my flesh longs for You in a dry and thirsty land where there is no water"* (Psalm 63:1 NKJV). David was not crying out for physical water; he was crying out for spiritual water because he was in a spiritual drought. One of the biblical symbols for the Word of God is water. David was in need of a word or an insight from the Lord, and he sought Him during "prime time," or early in the morning.

♦ The Miraculous One, Jesus Christ, placed the ultimate seal of approval on this pattern of interaction with the Father by practicing what is revealed in the passage below. The gospel of Mark records Jesus seeking His heavenly Father at almost exactly the same time of day that God spoke to the boy Samuel: *"In the early morning, while it was still dark, Jesus got up, left the house, and went away to a secluded place, and was praying there"* (Mark 1:35 NASB).

In each of the above passages, the writer detailed not only the event but also the time when it occurred. All the passages describe interactions with God during spiritual "prime time." Now, I am not dogmatic about this. I don't celebrate external form over intimate connection with the Father. In fact, I naturally tend to lean more toward the "organic" and spontaneous than I do the structured or routine. However, it is impossible to deny the benefits of a godly routine when attempting to come into or maintain our miraculous potential.

Thus, while it isn't necessary or wise to try to limit our seeking of the Lord to a certain hour of the day—the Bible has many examples of people seeking God at other times of the day—the early morning is a great time for the person on a path of spiritual discovery to learn to discern His voice. Without question, there are innumerable benefits to developing such a practice. Here are a few of them, starting with the most practical.

Early in the morning, there are normally fewer distractions, so when we need to experience unbroken/uninterrupted communication with God, this tends to be the ideal time. Most other people are asleep, daily business has not yet started, social media interaction is greatly reduced, and other interests or entertainments are less likely to compete for our attention. It is, without question, the prime real estate on the landscape of our day. There doesn't seem to be any other time within the daily, twenty-four-hour period that is as significant as the two-to-three-hour window of the early morning.

Second, seeking to hear from God early is significant because it may be the ideal hour for spiritual and even mental absorption (for certain types of retention). Neuroscience shows that our brain doesn't receive or store information the same way all day but performs best at peak times, depending on the task. In the mornings, immediate recall is at its highest. Evenings can be a better time for the brain to absorb copious amounts of information, based on the human body's circadian rhythms. But remember, God rarely speaks to us through lengthy discourse. Instead, He often speaks in seed form that increases in impact through greater illumination, conversation, or confirmation. In His supreme wisdom, God does not waste words. For our benefit—and sanity—He often gives His word in doses, like a time-release capsule. In this case, we have the word in its entirety when He gives it, but the depth of its effect on us is fully realized over time. In the morning, our minds and spirits are like new sponges, ready to absorb. However, by evening, they are completely saturated—not just with God's words but also with the content of conversations we've had with others, workplace frustrations, family issues, challenging social interactions, stress over mounting tasks, distracting mental images, and even dismay over the deplorably low number of social media "likes" we've received for a post we thought was amazing.

The early morning is a fresher time of day, especially if you've slept well, because sleep restores you both physically and mentally, and you have not yet been bombarded with the day's information overload or a mood-altering encounter with anyone. Your mornings set the trajectory for the next twelve to sixteen hours. Usually, the first thing your mind feeds on in the morning will permeate the rest of your day. That is why the first song you hear often ends up being stuck in your head, or why the first emotion you feel is so difficult to shake. If you want to increase the resonance of anything in your life, including an endeavor to hear God, do it early and often. Again, God doesn't limit His communications to the early morning, but they can be the clearest, the most prominent, and the most pronounced at that time because of our higher absorption rate.

Another reason our early mornings are to be guarded and treasured is that this period in our day can carry a unique grace. God honors our desires when we honor Him, and seeking our heavenly Father at an early hour honors Him. I don't think it's that He responds to the sacrifice of our rising early or to the suffering we may incur by the loss of an extra hour of sleep. Instead, I believe it honors Him because it brings us into alignment with the spiritual principle of "firstfruits." Today, many people associate the principle of giving our "firstfruits" to God with a televangelist's appeal for a monetary donation, but the concept applies much more broadly than the financial arena—it fills the pages of Scripture in various contexts. "Firstfruits" is a principle of paying honor to the Lord that states, in effect, "When we give God our first and best, He causes His favor to fall on the rest!"

I live by this principle, not because God mandates it but because it helps me to honor Him in every area of my life.

+ The "firstfruits" of my resources are my tithes and offerings to God. I have honored God with my monetary resources in this way since childhood. As I give my first and best to God's work, I trust Him to favor the rest.

+ The "firstfruits" of my week is Sunday, on which I am committed to participating in the corporate worship of God. While God can be worshipped at any time, anywhere, there is a personal principle of honor, toward God and toward others, that is cultivated in me every time I gather with fellow believers on the first day of the week. Though the practice of worshipping God on Sunday mornings should not be taught dogmatically or insisted upon (some very effective churches meet at alternative times weekly), I participate in this practice for the purpose of honoring the Lord with the "first and best" part of my week. While the "first" part of that equation is obvious, the "best" portion of the practice is experienced (by most who follow it) through the reality that Sunday is a "downtime day" and, usually, the day in which we can get the most rest after our five- or six-day work week. There is also historical precedence for worshipping on Sunday. After the first-century church eventually transitioned from daily to weekly gatherings, Sunday became the most common day for corporate worship (mostly because Sunday is associated with the day of the Lord's resurrection). Again, while it is not a biblical mandate, I have found tremendous benefit from beginning my week in the house of God. In many respects, it sets the trajectory for the other six days.

+ The "firstfruits" of my day is my early-morning prime time with God. It is my first and best time of the day, and when I meet God at that time, the later part of my waking hours seem to be unusually favored. This does not mean that challenges and difficulties don't arise, but even when they do, I seem to have a unique strength and fortitude in handling them. God not only speaks to me but also frequently gives me a "daily briefing" and revelation that would otherwise be unknown to me. For example, during this time, God has caused images of various friends and acquaintances who are in need or trouble to flash across my mind—images of people on the verge of divorce, suicide, extramarital affairs, or other significant compromises—without my having had any observable clues or empirical evidence about these situations. God has literally saved lives, resources, and relationships as I have responded to revelation given during those hours. Additionally, during my early-morning briefing, God has navigated me around political ambushes, prepared me for unkind experiences, and instructed me to capitalize on opportunities that would come later that day. While God could have revealed these things to me at any time, as I expressed previously, I find that I tend to receive more significant results with less effort during my "prime time."

After people understand the vital elements of posture and prime time, they may still have difficulties in hearing God because they lack experience in two additional areas: recognition and clarity. In the next chapter, we will explore these essentials by continuing to look at the life of Samuel.

7

RECOGNITION AND CLARITY

RECOGNIZING GOD'S VOICE

Even among mature believers, there seems to be much mystery and ambiguity surrounding the idea of hearing the voice of God. Many people feel that it is an almost impossible attainment, reserved only for the extremely gifted, prophetically savvy "Spirituals." But I want to emphasize again that the ability to hear from the Lord is accessible to every child of God.

The more I interact with people who believe it is very difficult to hear from the Lord, the more I see a certain pattern emerge. When I begin to ask them pointed questions and to describe the ways in which God communicates with His people, most of them have a "eureka" moment. They quickly discover that their issue isn't generally a problem with hearing but one of recognition. In fact, the overwhelming response I anticipate from readers of this book is not "I've never heard God" but "Oh, *that* was God!"

TRAINING TO HEAR

Think about Samuel's encounter with the Lord. When did God speak to him? Was it before or after Eli's instruction about

what he should do when the Lord spoke? Samuel actually heard
God speak three times before Eli explained what it was or gave him
any spiritual direction about it:

> Then the LORD called Samuel. Samuel answered, "Here I
> am." And he ran to Eli and said, "Here I am; you called me."
> But Eli said, "I did not call; go back and lie down." So he went
> and lay down. Again the LORD called, "Samuel!" And Samuel
> got up and went to Eli and said, "Here I am; you called me."
> "My son," Eli said, "I did not call; go back and lie down." Now
> Samuel did not yet know the LORD: the word of the LORD had
> not yet been revealed to him. A third time the LORD called,
> "Samuel!" And Samuel got up and went to Eli and said, "Here
> I am; you called me." Then Eli realized that the LORD was
> calling the boy. So Eli told Samuel, "Go and lie down, and if he
> calls you, say, 'Speak, LORD, for your servant is listening.'" So
> Samuel went and lay down in his place. The LORD came and
> stood there, calling as at the other times, "Samuel! Samuel!"
> Then Samuel said, "Speak, for your servant is listening."
>
> (1 Samuel 3:4–10)

Samuel clearly heard the voice of the Lord but attributed it to
something else within the realm of his limited understanding—he
thought it was the voice of Eli. It was only after Eli's instruction
that Samuel understood what to do with what he had already been
hearing.

Like Samuel, the vast majority of us need(ed) guidance and
instruction to have more confidence in recognizing the communication of our heavenly Father. Again, many people today have already
heard God's voice but have not realized what it was. As God seeks
to guide us, we often fail to recognize His communications because
we don't always know what we're listening (or looking) for, or even
how to identify it when it arrives. We can benefit from spiritual

teachers and coaches who patiently guide us and help to confirm that a word is from God. Even so, we should remember that good spiritual teachers never want to be the primary vessel through which God speaks to those they're helping to develop. Rather, they want God to use their teaching to prepare people to better hear His voice for themselves.

It has always been a bit curious to me that much of the religious culture of our day celebrates spiritual training in certain areas while essentially restricting it in others. We have no problem teaching people how to teach—an ability that is actually listed as a spiritual gift in Romans 12:6–8, 1 Corinthians 12:28, and Ephesians 4:11. But when it comes to instruction on hearing the voice of God, there is not as much emphasis or affirmation. Entire conferences are created to equip people to become more effective teachers, but you would be hard pressed to find many classes on fine-tuning your ear to hear God.

The above passage in 1 Samuel not only demonstrates our need for instruction in recognizing and accurately discerning God's voice, but also the necessity of having a teachable spirit if we want to participate in this process. Samuel was teachable, and he walked in enough humility to follow Eli's instruction. I believe that one of the impediments to greater encounters with God in our generation is people's inability to handle guidance or correction. Another significant challenge is that no one wants to appear as a novice in any context (even when they are). "Fake it till you make it, even if you never do" could easily be the motto that defines the disposition of the masses.

Furthermore, we often miss out on quality instruction in spiritual matters because the packaging it comes in doesn't always match our expectations. This is why most of the religious leaders in Jesus' day didn't recognize that the Messiah Himself was in their presence. We have a tendency to judge the quality of people's spiritual authority and wisdom by the wrong standards. We make people spiritual authorities based on the size of their churches, their current popularity, or even their personal charisma, but we should ask, "Do they have an intimate relationship with God, and have they learned to hear from Him?"

In a related way, we often miss great instruction by focusing on the frailty of the vessel that bears it rather than receiving instruction out of that person's area of strength. I'm sure Samuel could have found an inconsistency or two in his mentor Eli that would have given him the wiggle room to discredit him and his instruction. After all, the high priest couldn't keep his wicked sons under control, and he didn't prevent them from eating the fat portions of sacrifices that were meant to be dedicated to the Lord. Yet Eli still knew enough about God to instruct others on hearing His voice. He wasn't giving Samuel instruction on parenting or how to discipline his appetites but on how to recognize the voice of the Lord. It takes humility to receive instruction from someone who has superior insights in one particular area when you have qualities that are far superior to theirs in other areas; yet Samuel followed Eli's instruction and was the better for it.

Having a humble and teachable spirit will bring us into greater truth and increase our ability to hear and recognize God's voice. I think there was a particular reason why Samuel's encounter with the Lord's voice happened while he was still a youth and in the impressionable years of his life. The historian Josephus puts him at approximately twelve years of age at this time. I am convinced that his age has a revelation contained in it concerning our ability to hear the Lord: people who are best positioned to receive fresh revelation from God are those who approach Him not as seasoned experts but as children. Jesus said, *"Truly I tell you, unless you change and become like little children, you will never enter the kingdom of heaven. Therefore, whoever takes the lowly position of this child is the greatest in the kingdom of heaven"* (Matthew 18:3–4).

In God's kingdom, our humility increases our receptivity. I remember adamantly arguing theological points with people who were experiencing spiritual realities that I, too, longed to experience. My areas of expertise, my religious formation, my denominational affiliation, and my spiritual pride would not allow me to be instructed by them. I debated the "Eli's" God brought into my life because I viewed reality through the lenses of my limited experiences, instead of hearing the perspectives of those who had already experienced what I wanted to.

As long as the instruction is biblical, the person with the experience always trumps the person with the theory. For example, I don't want someone who's merely read a book on aeronautics to be my flight instructor but rather one who has read the book *and* logged hours of successful flight. Again, the one with both theory and experience outranks the one with theory alone. And humility is the quality that allows us to recognize which one we are in any given situation and to adjust ourselves accordingly.

I imagine Samuel going back to bed after being given the instruction from Eli. He knows now that he's not crazy or delusional—he's not "hearing voices." The voice he heard previously was not of human origin but rather of divine origin. It was the voice of the great God of all. I'm taking interpretive liberties, but I picture Samuel lying down in his place, gripped by wonder like a child on Christmas Eve, awaiting another utterance. The simple insight here is the importance of being expectant. Begin every day expecting to hear the voice of the Lord and to receive His guidance. We so often miss what we're not looking for. Keep a writing or typing instrument close and go before God daily with eager anticipation; He will not disappoint!

THE IMPORTANCE OF PLACE

Because we live in a culture of sensory overload, it's no wonder that we struggle to hear the voice of the Lord with clarity. While

I am not anti-technology or anti-entertainment, I am pro-spiritual intimacy, and at times the former stands in opposition to the latter. In addition to our constant communications through e-mails, text messages, voicemail, and multiple social media accounts, which alert us to new communications by the second, most of us are, frankly, consumed with our entertainment options. Today, there aren't just a few well-written shows or movies on network television to draw our attention in our spare time. Now, hundreds of enticing cable TV programs and Internet-based shows are available at all times of the day, so the options are endless. Even the landscape of sports and the attention given to it has become more consuming. With developments like Fantasy Football, people are no longer occasionally watching a home game featuring "their" team but keeping up with multiple teams and their progress throughout the year to stay competitive. Entertainment has become a major fixture in our lives.

Additional stimulation is provided by advertisers who study the human psyche, appetite, and behavioral patterns and intentionally plant emotional and psychological bait with hooks in the form of TV commercials, Internet pop-ups, electronic billboards, and more. While we've already established the fact that God can speak to us at any time and under any circumstance, clarity becomes a challenge when multiple distractions compete for the same mental, spiritual, and emotional space.

Consequently, while the posture of the heart, teachability, and designating a specific period of time to seek God are essential elements in the life of someone who desires to clearly discern God's voice, we cannot overlook the importance of an additional, related factor—"place." The Scriptures say that after being instructed by Eli about the voice of God, *"Samuel went and lay down in his* **place***"* (1 Samuel 3:9). I don't believe there are any wasted revelations in this passage. Samuel was now trained, primed, and postured to receive heavenly instruction, but part of what made that possible was his physical place, or proximity to God, a place of quiet and solitude.

Where was Samuel? He was *"in the house of the LORD, where the ark of God was"* (1 Samuel 3:3). Most probably, this statement doesn't imply that he slept on the ground right next to the ark of the covenant. Instead, he was in his own designated room. In the tabernacle where the ark was, there were chambers with beds for the priests to sleep in. It was there, without distractions and with a reasonable amount of solitude, that Samuel received the instruction of the Lord with crystal clarity.

I want to reemphasize that God does not need His children to be in isolation to get a word through to them. However, being in a quiet place, absent of distraction, does help tremendously when we are learning to hear God, fine-tuning our ability to hear, recalibrating our spiritual sensitivity, or in need of heightened clarity. Like the practice of Jesus and the early disciples, seeking God in solitude can aid us in hearing His voice more clearly. Dallas Willard, in his book *The Spirit of the Disciplines*, credits much of the first-century church's miraculous existence to the disciplines they employed, one of which was solitude. He writes, "All of those who followed Jesus knew of his practice of solitude, and it was greatly imitated in the centuries after his death."[3]

Regarding the importance of solitude in Jesus' life, Willard says,

> Jesus constantly sought solitude from the time of his baptism up to the Garden of Gethsemane, when he even went apart from those he took there to watch with him (Matt. 26: 38–42). It is solitude and solitude alone that opens the possibility of a radical relationship to God that can withstand all external events up to and beyond death.

3. Dallas Willard, *The Spirit of the Disciplines: Understanding How God Changes Lives* (New York: Harper Collins, 1988), 102.

Retirement is the laboratory of the spirit; interior solitude and silence are its two wings. All great works are
prepared in the desert, including the redemption of the
world.[4]

As Samuel lay in his *"place,"* the God of heaven spoke to him—
confirming a previous prophetic word given to Eli—that the order
of the priesthood in Israel would be altered: Eli and his wicked
sons would be judged and removed. Subsequently, Samuel would
be established as the next priest of Israel. (See 1 Samuel 2:27–36;
3:11–14.)

Like Samuel, in times of solitude, I, too, have received unique
insights from the Lord. As a result of those moments, I have
received not only open doors of opportunity, but also successful
business concepts and life-altering insights for my family. Sadly,
we often miss significant opportunities that would have resulted
from God's communications to us because we neglect or refuse to
meet Him in our own places of solitude. In these cases, the loss is
always ours.

DEVOTION PLUS SERVICE

When we consider the principle of solitude, a balanced perspective is warranted. After discovering this principle, some people
go to extremes and attempt to live lives of virtual isolation in devotion to the Lord. The only problem is that God requires not only
our dedication to Him but also our service and ministry to humanity. We are meant to be the instruments through which He flows to
touch the other inhabitants of this world, whom He deeply loves.
In fact, Jesus essentially condensed the totality of the Scriptures
into the following statements: *"Love the Lord your God with all your
heart and with all your soul and with all your mind and with all your*

---

4. Ibid., 101.

strength" and "*Love your neighbor as yourself.*" (See Mark 12:28–31.) God's intent is always to draw His children vertically toward Him and horizontally toward one another. We are drawn toward Him in devotion and toward others in service. A passage in 1 John illustrates this link more strongly by suggesting that our relationships to God and humanity are inextricably connected:

> *We love, because He first loved us. If someone says, "I love God," and hates his brother, he is a liar; for the one who does not love his brother whom he has seen, cannot love God whom he has not seen. And this commandment we have from Him, that the one who loves God should love his brother also.*
>
> (1 John 4:19–21 NASB)

No one reconciled and exemplified these realities better than Jesus. He demonstrated an unwavering devotion and connection to the Father. Luke 22:39 (NASB) says, "[Jesus] *came out and proceeded as was His custom to the Mount of Olives.*" The phrase "*as was His custom*" refers to something done according to routine or habit. This verse reveals that Jesus regularly got away from His ministry to the crowds in order to commune with the Father. In other words, *He habitually practiced solitude.*

Yet He not only regularly practiced solitude but also used it to harness the miraculous for the people whom He would serve. It was because He had been with the Father in that place of solitude on the Mount of Olives that He was able to minister to the needs of humanity. As He functioned in His anointed humanity, He set a pattern for us to follow. He was showing us, among other things, that we cannot expect to add value to the crowd if we are always among the crowd. However, if we are never among people, the grace of God through us to them becomes limited.

In Luke 21, there is a passage that further reveals the relationship between Jesus' communion with God (in solitude) and His ministry to people (in public):

> *During the day He was teaching in the temple, but at eve-*
> *ning He would go out and spend the night on the mount that*
> *is called Olivet. And all the people would get up early in the*
> *morning to come to Him in the temple to listen to Him.*
>
> (Luke 21:37–38 NASB)

Christ received the Father's insights, instruction, refreshing, and greater direction in those times of intimacy. He came down from the mountain with the choicest morsels of heaven to feed humanity's hungry souls, and we are still feasting today on the revelation He received from the Father in solitude. If we are to realize our miraculous potential, periods of uninterrupted solitude and communion with the Father must not be neglected.

8

FAITH, FLEXIBILITY, AND ACTION

Before exploring the specific ways God speaks, we will need to consider some of the practical points that will support our encounters with His voice. In this chapter, we will discover the roles of faith, flexibility, and action in hearing God. Then, in the following chapter, we will learn the advantage of becoming familiar with the multiple ways the Lord speaks.

EXERCISING FAITH

At the heart of every one of our encounters with God, including hearing from Him, is the necessity of faith. In fact, the Bible specifically states, *"Without faith it is impossible to please God"* (Hebrews 11:6). But it takes faith for us to even understand the definition of faith, which is stated at the beginning of Hebrews 11: *"Faith is the substance of things hoped for, the evidence of things not seen"* (verse 1 NKJV, KJV). Built into this description is a paradox; it contains concepts that seem to be polar-opposites and that can only be reconciled in this context alone. Two of the descriptive terms signify something concrete, and two of them signify something abstract. Faith is referred to as *"substance"* and *"evidence"* (the concrete aspects), yet the substance is *"hoped for"* and the evidence is *"unseen"* (the abstract aspects).

This definition of faith therefore carries both clarity and ambiguity. In light of this, I would like to point out something that, if not recognized, causes many people to misunderstand the nature of our heavenly Father and His ways: in regard to God and His knowledge, there are certain things He reveals and certain things He keeps veiled, at least in our present time. For this reason, in our relationship with Him, there are things that we currently know, and there are other things we have yet to grasp. This is one way in which God maintains His intimacy with us while retaining His mystery.

The apostle Paul emphasized this reality when he wrote, *"For we know in part and we prophesy in part; but when the perfect comes, the partial will be done away"* (1 Corinthians 13:9–10 NASB). While I have set my heart on the daily pursuit of knowing God more, I also rest in the reality of this mystery. And I know I will never experience a complete unveiling of all of His knowledge or counsel until my life on earth—or this age of humanity—is over. As long as we live in this world, there will be reasonable limitations to our knowledge about God and to the revelation we receive from Him. We won't fully grasp the infinite depths of God's mind until we see Him face-to-face. Paul continued the above passage by saying that in that day, we *"will know fully* [with no limitations] *just as* [we] *also have been fully known* [by God]" (1 Corinthians 13:12 NASB)—but until then, we must exercise faith.

Faith is what closes the chasm between mystery and revelation by allowing us to function without always having full disclosure. Our faith is what grants us permission to move forward with what is revealed without being hindered by what is not yet unveiled. To make significant strides in God's kingdom, we must be prepared to progress by combining strong conviction with the temporary agony of uncertainty. Many people experience frustrations while attempting to exercise their faith because they follow the instructions or listen to the testimonies of those who downplay their uncertainty while embellishing their confidence.

So, as we seek to hear and obey, we should remember that with God, there is much that can be known, but there will always be unknown variables. No matter how "spiritual" or "seasoned" we are, receiving what God is saying requires a measure of faith, because while we may possess strong convictions concerning His leading, we are rarely guaranteed a 100 percent confirmation before we acknowledge and act on that leading. We still *"know in part"* and will at times question whether we're really hearing God or being led by Him. We will ask ourselves, for example, *Did that word come from God, or did it come from my own selfish motivations?* (We will address this question more fully in a later chapter.)

If God could be fully grasped within the limitations of our human understanding, He wouldn't be a God who is infinitely beyond us. People who are perfectionists or "controlaholics" have pronounced difficulty with this fact because they require full disclosure or predictable outcomes before taking action. Of course, there are times when God may communicate in a more dramatic way, bringing various types of overt revelations or manifestations. In these moments, some things that were "hoped for" are realized and some things that were "unseen" are revealed to us. However, God's method of disclosure is usually to provide what is needed for us to take action right now, while He maintains a degree of the unknown, requiring us to continually depend on and trust Him. His desire is to grant us revelation that fosters continual relationship, and this is just one of the reasons that faith will always be required when it comes to hearing the voice of God and acting on it.

REMAINING FLEXIBLE

In addition to faith, the quality of flexibility is needed. After obeying utterances believed to be from God, many people commonly experience disappointment and confusion over unmet expectations. How many times have we responded to what we thought was the leading of God, only to find there was no dramatic confirmation, reward, or apparent reason for it? I call these moments (from a human perspective) "divine dead ends"—steps of faith that don't seem to yield any obvious fruit.

The first and only time I heard what I believe was the audible voice of God, I was still in high school living with my grandparents. Like Samuel, I attributed the voice to someone in the house calling me. However, after getting up a few times to search out the source of the voice, I realized I was alone on that side of the home. It was then that I looked to God for clarity. At that moment, the same voice uttered words I will never forget: "Go to the beach."

With goose bumps running all over my body and anticipation consuming me, I immediately responded to this voice of authority. In fact, I was so enraptured with the command that I ran to the other side of the house and hastily told my grandparents, "God told me to go to the beach!" They responded with excitement because they were people of faith and were thrilled that I was having any type of interaction with God. Up to that moment, I don't think there was any prominent evidence of His work in my life.

As I started down the stairs, propelled by urgency, my grandmother offered me her car keys to help facilitate my obedient response. However, I was so obsessed with the divine instruction that I refused her offer and grabbed a bike at the bottom of the stairs because it was closer and (to my excited mind) would allow me to respond more quickly. It wasn't until I had peddled halfway to my destination and my mind had caught up to the condition of my spirit that I realized it probably would have been faster and easier to take my grandmother's truck. After another ten minutes of mad peddling, I arrived at my destination.

Because I had heard such a dramatic communication from God, I now expected to experience something unusual, extraordinary, and miraculous! Would God part the waters as He had for Moses and Joshua? Would He literally open the heavens as He had for Jesus? Would He bring me to the water's edge and let me defy the laws of physics by walking on water in order to build my faith? I stepped onto the beach toward the shoreline and looked for further instruction or confirmation. It was at that moment that God said... nothing. I walked further toward where the water met the sand, figuring I would give the "water walk" a try but ended up with no testimony—just wet shoes.

I waited on that beach for hours, hoping for a last-minute divine moment or maybe a revelation concerning what this dramatic encounter had all been about, but I never received it. After a considerable amount of time, I jumped back on my bike, bewildered, and peddled with wet socks all the way home. When I got back, to add injury to insult, those who had seen me leave in anticipation and holy reverence saw me come back in discouragement. I had no report or testimony of the miraculous origin of the word, only a divine dead end!

Whether or not you've ever had a similar experience, I'm sure you can relate to having had unmet expectations associated with following what you believed to be God's leading. Experiences such as these are actually vital to our continued development in the things of God. Depending on our response to them, they can either make us—further our effectiveness—or break us—limit our effectiveness.

It is at such a point that many people conclude, "I didn't hear from God," "God made a fool out of me, and I won't be made a fool of again," or "There are too many risks associated with following God's voice—it's easier to live a life of well-managed and predictable spirituality." They misunderstand the nature of these divine dead ends and therefore opt out of divine leading altogether in exchange for "safe," static tradition or principles.

Having taken the above mentioned leap of faith and falling flat, I am intimately familiar with their frustration. However, in the midst of my discouragement, I found an encouraging insight in the book of Jeremiah regarding God's communications to us and these apparent dead ends. In this passage, which I believe shows us that divine dead ends are nothing new, the Lord sheds a bit of light on their necessity in our lives. Here are His words to the prophet Jeremiah in the seventh century BC:

> *The word of the Lord came to me: "What do you see, Jeremiah?" "I see the branch of an almond tree," I replied. The Lord said to me, "You have seen correctly, for I am watching to see that my word is fulfilled." The word of the Lord came to me again: "What do you see?" "I see a pot that is boiling," I answered. "It is tilting toward us from the north." The Lord said to me, "From the north disaster will be poured out on all who live in the land."* (Jeremiah 1:11–14)

Looking at the structure of this passage, we find four verses containing two distinct words to Jeremiah. Verses 11 and 12 contain the first utterance of God, and verses 13 and 14 the second. In my view, the first utterance of God to Jeremiah could be considered a divine dead end in that nothing seemed to happen in relation to it. The Lord showed the prophet a vision, asked what he saw, and then simply told him He was watching over His word. There was no significant insight, prophecy, or meaning associated with His first word to Jeremiah. In essence, God was saying, "I wanted to see that you could see/hear and respond to Me." So perhaps the Lord's intent was merely to test Jeremiah's ability to correctly hear and respond, or to familiarize him further with His voice and visions. It might have been a training of sorts, a grooming of the vessel and a proving of his fitness to handle further instruction. If nothing else, it was a reminder from the Lord that sometimes words come to us absent of specific meaning but never without a purpose.

Jeremiah passed the first round. He proved not only that he could spiritually see, hear, and respond but also that he stood ready to hear and respond again to a God who had just spoken a word that had no apparent significance for him. This demonstrated Jeremiah's internal resolve to respond to God's voice whether there was clarity or uncertainty attached to His communication. It seems Jeremiah didn't see God's test as a point of contention or discouragement but as an opportunity to continue to fine-tune his ability to hear. When God finds someone with that type of trust and resolve, He entrusts them with more of His instructions and also with divine fruit, or results.

The Lord next spoke in a similar manner; but this time, meaning and significance were attached! Let's reread that part of the encounter:

> The word of the LORD came to me again: "What do you see?" "I see a pot that is boiling," I answered. "It is tilting toward us from the north." The LORD said to me, "From the north disaster will be poured out on all who live in the land."
>
> (Jeremiah 1:13–14)

In this second communication, God didn't speak to test Jeremiah's response but to share His divine mind, which contained what would unfold in the future for Jeremiah's region of the world. I believe this passage further reveals for us the need for flexibility as we learn to hear (or continue to hear) and respond to the voice of God. Sometimes His instructions are immediately fruitful and come packaged with full understanding, but other times no clear results are produced.

If there is one thing that can sabotage or undermine the next word from God to you, it is a previous word that didn't pan out the way you expected it to. Like Jeremiah, we must have flexibility, resilience, and a mind-set that realizes that even when God's instruction doesn't appear to be fruitful, it's always purposeful. Again, if we refuse to give in to bitterness and discouragement, and stay adaptable even in uncertainty, God will entrust to us greater divine direction and the results that follow it.

My experience at the beach appeared fruitless to me at the time, yet later I realized it was part of my training ground in hearing God, accomplishing these results: (1) It taught me to hear and respond to the voice of God and served as a dramatic prophetic sign marking a life dedicated to bringing others into the same reality. (2) It taught me the importance of staying open to God even after a frustrating experience with His voice, which is a quality every servant of God should possess. After all, if my service and receptivity toward Him are limited to times of encouragement, my effectiveness will be partial at best. (3) It taught me that obedience to God doesn't always come with full disclosure. Like Job, who had no idea about the heavenly realities affecting his earthly circumstances, or like the prophets, who spoke oracles that were manifested hundreds and even thousands of years after their own lifetimes, we in our own time must be trained in the art of divine obedience that does not require complete disclosure.

When our heavenly Father finds men and women who are flexible enough to give Him the latitude to be God, He begins to show them things "eyes have not seen and ears have not heard"! (See 1 Corinthians 2:9.)

TAKING ACTION

This is an age when the proliferation of information is at an all-time high. We are drawn to news, facts, data, and concepts, and many people feel a sense of empowerment when they grasp a new idea or mentally master a complex issue. In contrast, "mastery" of divinely-inspired communications is not measured by mental absorption but by personal response and activity. It is not simply acknowledging a truth as accurate but adjusting one's entire life and actions based on that acknowledged truth.

When God gives us information and other revelation, He desires not only that we hear what He has spoken but also that we respond appropriately to it; He expects that we will receive it and take responsibility for what we have heard. The nature of our response will either open the floodgates of revelation or limit the divine conversation. Jesus elaborated on this idea in Matthew 13, a portion of which we looked at in an earlier chapter. He had just related the parable of the sower, and in response to a question from His disciples about why He spoke in parables (divine stories with hidden meaning until explained or interpreted), Jesus said,

> *Because the knowledge of the secrets of the kingdom of heaven has been given to you, but not to them* [the crowds]. *Whoever has will be given more, and they will have an abundance. Whoever does not have, even what they have will be taken from them. This is why I speak to them in parables: "Though seeing, they do not see; though hearing, they do not hear or understand."*   (Matthew 13:11–13)

This passage reveals a couple of interesting points in relation to hearing from God. The first is that we see two groups here— one group that received limited disclosure from God (the crowds) and the other that received full disclosure, along with ongoing communication with Him (the disciples). But what is even more interesting is Jesus' explanation of why—outside of their heart position, which we dealt with previously—those in the first group were not entrusted with divine knowledge or further revelation.

To emphasize His point, Jesus declared, *"Whoever has will be given more, and they will have an abundance. Whoever does not have, even what they have will be taken from them."*

Jesus made exactly the same statements later on in Matthew's gospel at the end of the parable of the talents in relation to the integrity of our stewardship, or what we do with that which is entrusted to our care by God. (See Matthew 25:14–30.) The parable in Matthew 25 illustrates the principle of stewardship by using the monetary currency of Jesus' time. I believe, however, that the stewardship described is not of money alone but of everything God has given us, including revelations, insights, and other words from Him. In this parable, three servants are entrusted with a certain amount of money from their master. The first servant receives five talents, the second receives two, and the third receives one. The servant who receives five talents trades with them and makes five more; the servant who receives two talents likewise trades with what he was given and doubles his investment; but the servant who receives the single talent does nothing with his portion except bury it for safekeeping. When the master returns, he congratulates the servants who did something with what he gave them, but he rebukes the one who did nothing with his portion. In fact, the master takes that one talent and gives it to the servant who has ten. Again, at the conclusion of the parable, we find the same lines that we read previously in Matthew 13: *"Whoever has will be given more, and they will have an abundance. Whoever does not have, even what they have will be taken from them"* (Matthew 25:29).

In my view, Jesus was making a clear-cut connection between the parable of the talents and the results associated with how we handle His Word, His insights, or His revelations when He repeated the statement He previously gave following the parable of the sower (*"Whoever has will be given more"*) as He taught on revelation from God. For those who bury His revelations in the recesses of their minds and never do anything with them, the flow of revelation is taken away. However, for those who do something with the revelations they receive, more are lavished on them.

I have experienced this reality is my own life. When I don't do anything with the previous words or revelations God has given me, I am hindered from receiving fresh revelations and from experiencing a constant flow of communications from the Lord. While I'm in this position, what God speaks to me is rarely new information but rather encouragement to put into practice what He's already told me. One of the first questions I ask myself when there seems to be drought of God's speaking is, *Are there words God has already spoken or things He's already led me to do that I haven't moved on yet?* If there are, I obediently respond to them, and I often receive new insights in the days that follow. The one who does something with what God speaks is always replenished with fresh words.

Before Father's Day a couple of years ago, I looked all over town to find a fitting gift for my father. In one department store, a pushy salesman asked what I was shopping for. When I told him Father's Day, he insisted that I should buy a complete state-of-the-art tool set, which he declared was a must-have because it was half price for that week only. When I declined his offer, he looked dumbfounded. Thinking I misheard him, he commenced to repeat his entire pitch, except this time he ended with the statement, "Any man would appreciate this gift." Once I realized this salesman wasn't backing off, I remained calm but became more firm. I told him that I completely understood this was "the deal of a lifetime" but that it would be a complete waste of valuable resources (both my money and the tools). I went on to explain that in my lifetime, I'd never seen my father build anything. Though the tool set looked like a quality product, my concluding statement was, "It would be foolish to give him a gift I know he'll never use." My father wouldn't have appreciated it, and my investment would have been squandered. Similarly,

God rarely continues to entrust His valuable words and revelation to individuals who will never obediently respond to them.

Temporal gifts are not always valuable to the recipients, depending on people's interests and preference, but God's communications to us are always of tremendous worth and significance. The heavenly Father is looking for those who recognize the value of His investment in them, to the degree that revelation produces action. His words are not designed to make you smarter but to construct heavenly realities on earth. This is why an abundance of revelation isn't given to the mental hoarder but rather to the faithful steward who is willing to construct something by obeying what he or she hears.

9

INCREASED BANDWIDTH

Both the Old and New Testaments are filled with accounts of heavenly communications to men and women. Under the new covenant in Christ, it is primarily the indwelling Holy Spirit who keeps us intimately connected to the Father, but words from God can come in many forms and varied expressions.

MULTIPLE OUTLETS OF COMMUNICATION

The Holy Spirit has multiple means of communicating with us—but many believers are ignorant of these methods or dismiss them as unnecessary. Still others believe that employing any communications method other than the Bible undermines the authority of Scripture in our lives. I believe this view stems from a profound misunderstanding of the nature of God and how He communicates. All these methods work synergistically and cohesively toward one goal because the Source is the same: God is the driving force behind them all. We can be assured that if any guidance, prompting, or communication violates the Bible (the ultimate standard), it is not from God and should be dismissed; but if it complements God's Word and finds agreement with His Spirit, it is to be accepted and utilized.

BENEFITS OF GOD'S COMMUNICATION OUTLETS

A GREATER RANGE OF SPIRITUAL FREQUENCY

God desires to place at our disposal various outlets of communication so that we can experience greater receptivity to His words. Before we explore these multiple tools in detail in the next several chapters, we should be aware of their purposes and advantages. The following illustration should help. In the early days of surfing the Internet, a traditional phone line with a wall jack and a connecting cord had to be used. The cord needed to be attached to a second phone jack built into the side of the computer. If someone was online, no one else in the house was able to use the phone, and the mobility of the person using the computer was limited to the length of the phone cord. In addition, the average Web page could take anywhere from ten seconds to two minutes to load, based on the content, and there were no options for upgrading. Today, when I listen to my son complain that the WiFi connection to his wireless iPad is taking a few seconds longer than usual, it's a testament to how far we've progressed technologically over the past twenty years.

The evolution of technology has been remarkable, involving considerable advances in speed, efficiency, and greater flexibility (mobility/range). And what made that increased performance possible was greater *bandwidth*. While this term is used in several ways today in relation to technology, I refer to the range of frequencies in a given band, especially one used for transmitting a signal. In the days of a single telephone cord for Internet use, information was transmitted more slowly due to the smaller band of fibers or limited wires transferring the information from the online source to our computers. However, when broadband and DSL (digital subscriber line) were introduced, bandwidth was increased, and communication efficiency was enhanced. The content, source, and receiver remained the same, but with more fibers/wires to transmit the data, the process became more seamless. The entire system was enhanced because there were more wires to create a greater range of frequencies.

Similarly, understanding the multiple ways God speaks to us can increase our "spiritual bandwidth," enabling us to better receive His communications. When we become aware of God's multiple means of expression and give Him the latitude to use any or all of them, we decrease our communication downtime and increase our communication efficiency. We enhance our awareness of His utterances with every biblically-consistent information outlet we make available for Him to use. Accessing only one or two lines of communication may still yield the same heavenly download (message) as the multiple-line approach—but probably not as rapidly, consistently, or compellingly.

Let me give you a simple example. Suppose God wants you, as a single person, to leave your home in Atlanta for a new start in Los Angeles. It would mean a serious step of faith for you because your family, friends, church, and job are all in Atlanta. While you have received an internal prompting about it from the Lord—a form of divine communication—you still have quite a few reservations because it would be a life-altering change. As a result, you deliberate a bit longer before making a decision whether to move or to stay.

Now, picture the same scenario with an additional variable. You have felt the original prompting from God to move from Atlanta to Los Angeles—a faith step that would require leaving your family, friends, church, and job. However, this time, as you're processing this prompting, you keep alert for other ways in which God may confirm this leading. The next Sunday morning, you hear a message at church about Abraham leaving his comfort zone (his hometown and his father's family) to trust God and travel to a new place. Then, after the service, one of the ministry team members stops to tell you about a dream she had of you in a new and unfamiliar place, but blessed beyond your wildest dreams. When you arrive at work the next day, the discussion in the staff meeting is about your company downsizing. And just to show His eye for detail, God allows the topic of your midweek Bible study group to be on how He sometimes confirms His word to us through the prompting of the Holy Spirit, the preached Word, confirming dreams, open and closed doors, and Bible study!

I think we could safely say you should make plans to move, give your two-week notice at work, and kiss your family and friends good-bye as you head to LA.

In both scenarios, the Source of the guidance was the same: God. In both, the instruction was the same: "Move from Atlanta to Los Angeles." In both, the recipient of the word was the same: you. However, the added variable was increased bandwidth. You sought and recognized more lines of communication from God. The content was the same, but with the increased bandwidth, the message came with greater clarity and effectiveness, and more compellingly. Many people regularly labor to hear God, not because He isn't speaking but because they have yet to upgrade their connection to Him by seeking—using biblical methods—the various ways in which He may be communicating with them.

THE ELIMINATION OF "DEAD ZONES"

I grew up in a large family (one member shy of the Brady Bunch), and on holidays and during summer vacations we took long road trips. What made these trips especially challenging was that our main forms of entertainment were guessing games, cards, and sing-alongs. After a couple of hours of playing "Concentration" and singing "99 Bottles of Beer on the Wall," we were ready to drive off the closest bridge. To keep our sanity, we would ask my mom to turn on the radio so we could listen to music. But finding a station we liked with good reception often proved to be difficult as we crossed into new and often desolate territory where little was being broadcast. Then there were parts of the country where we could get absolutely no reception. We called these areas "dead zones." There was nothing we could do but keep switching from FM to AM in hopes of finding some station. Changing frequencies sometimes solved the problem, but most times it did not.

Today's road-trip passengers rarely encounter dead zones in their search for electronic entertainment, as many vehicles come equipped not only with FM and AM radio but also satellite radio, mobile Internet radio, and vehicle WiFi. If one frequency is weak, there are several others that can be employed. Likewise, the more we become aware of the multiple communication outlets God uses to speak with us and to confirm His instruction and guidance, the better the frequency will be for hearing from heaven, and the less time we will spend wandering through spiritual dead zones where we don't feel we are hearing anything at all from God. While no amount of devotion to God or spiritual discipline can ensure unimpeded, round-the-clock revelation from Him, an understanding of His various methods of communication helps keep the lines open and lessens our sense of uncertainty.

THE BUILDING UP OF THE BODY OF CHRIST

A third benefit of understanding the multiple ways God speaks relates more to the community of faith than to the individual believer. In his second letter to Timothy, Paul instructed, *"The things you have heard me say in the presence of many witnesses entrust to reliable people who will also be qualified to teach others"* (2 Timothy 2:2). All of our spiritual advancements in the kingdom are to be shared with others in order to bring them into similar growth and progress in the faith. We therefore have an obligation to help others learn what we have discovered about hearing from God.

I have observed many people's spiritual formation, and one of the challenges I have noted is that the students tend to inherit both the strengths and the limitations of their teachers, whether the students have been expressly taught them or have learned them through observation and imitation. For instance, when leaders are personally sensitive to or have a preference for a particular type of communication from God, that style tends to be what they display or emphasize. The people in proximity to these leaders generally adopt that style rather than exploring other expressions of God's communication or learning the primary style He may want to use with them. This presents no real issue when those who tend to receive dreams from God, for example, are being mentored by someone who has the same bent. The challenge comes when the "dreamers" don't make those under their tutelage aware of other ways in which God speaks, such as through pictures, dominant thoughts, or the peace of the Holy Spirit.

Again, God reserves the right to use any medium He chooses to communicate with us, and He desires that we be aware of as many of such avenues as possible. He has also wired the body of Christ with tremendous diversity. Once they understand these principles, most people discover that God uses a unique method or primary style of communication with them. Therefore, knowing the multiple ways in which God speaks, as well as their own prominent leaning, protects people from having their receptivity limited to a teacher's personal style or inclination. It also helps to make them aware of the style of heavenly reception they may be primarily wired for.

In institutions of higher learning, students are typically trained at first with a broad education, and as time goes on, they narrow their program of study to a particular field or specialty, as they decide on a major that suits their strengths. Although they have a specified major, they can still draw on what they learned from the general core curriculum, finding it a helpful resource for the remainder of their schooling and even for the rest of their lives. Likewise, being trained in the multiple ways God speaks has all the benefits in the world and no detriments. Broadening your scope equips you to more accurately discern His speaking.

In the next few chapters, we will survey particular ways in which God spoke to His people in the Scriptures and how He still speaks today. As we do, let us realize that God's speaking to us, and our ability to hear Him, are necessary components to releasing our miraculous potential, because without these foundational elements, this God-produced existence would be unattainable for us.

10

HOW GOD SPEAKS, PART 1
THE BIBLE, THE HOLY SPIRIT, AND PEACE

Our goal is to be strengthened in the pursuit of knowing God—not just cognitively but experientially. If we desire to discern God's voice more accurately and more often, it is vital that we familiarize ourselves with the multiple ways He communicates. It's not my purpose here to create a theological defense for the fact that God speaks to us in various ways but to help the reader truly recognize His voice, and to promote confidence in such encounters. For this reason, in the next few chapters, I have included testimonies about hearing from God that are compatible with the authority of Scripture and that I hope will be an encouragement to you. As I wrote earlier, I wouldn't want a flight instructor who'd only read the flight manual but had no actual experience flying; I'd want someone with proven experience teaching me the manual and also sitting next to me in the cockpit as I learned to pilot the plane. A teacher needs to have tasted of the morsels he or she is offering.

In church or in everyday conversation, we often hear believers say, "God said…," "The Lord spoke to me…," "God told me…," or "God led me to…"—but is hearing from Him in this way really possible? If so, how does it happen? What these believers are trying to express is that God has somehow transferred information to them. Since this process can be confusing to many people (and because we all can be prone to error in such matters), I want to be clear about what I mean when I refer to the ways God speaks to us.

As I mentioned earlier, a number of believers have already heard God's voice or experienced His personal leading but, like Samuel, haven't fully recognized it as God. You may be one of them, so let me try to bring clarity by confirming some experiences you may have already had, as well as revealing possibilities you have yet to experience. My prayer is that we all will understand better what it means to hear God's voice in "high definition."

THE BIBLE

An excellent starting point in learning to hear the voice of God is the Bible, our standard for soundness. God speaks in fresh ways to every generation, and the voice of the Holy Spirit is as active today as it was two thousand years ago in the first-century church. However, it is important that we recognize—as the early church did, possessing the Old Testament and also the emerging writings of the New Testament—that the Bible is the God-approved compilation of divine utterances over the course of thousands of years.

God's Word speaks to the kinds of circumstances that confront people of all eras—not just those whose lives are highlighted in the biblical accounts. When we study the Bible, therefore, we are immediately privy to God's counsel on many matters that we deal with today, without having to endure a "dead zone" in relation to them. Before we try to discern the more abstract guidance of the Lord, it is always beneficial to get a handle on what He has established as concrete truths and principles through the pages of Scripture. God's Word—when read in context and with proper application—is the only avenue through which God speaks that cannot be trumped by any other authority, insight, or revelation, even if it is believed to be from God. Every human teaching, prophecy, or revelation should be investigated or weighed, and then either retained if confirmed or disregarded if found to be inconsistent with Scripture.

In Acts 17, we read about the Bereans, who listened gladly to the teachings of the apostles but then went home to study the Scriptures for themselves to see if the things they had been taught were true. Also, in 1 Corinthians 14, we see that Paul instructed the local church on how to weigh the words of prophets who had apparent messages from the Lord. These examples show us that people's teaching of the Bible or declaration of a prophetic word can be evaluated to determine whether it should be received or rejected. However, the revealed Word of God, or Scripture— again, in proper context and application—is never to be rejected, as it provides trustable, objective revelation and a standard by which all subjective revelation can be judged.

What God speaks to you today (subjectively) will not violate what He has spoken previously through His written Word (objectively). The Source is the same, and He is not duplicitous. This is why the Word is such a great resource for hearing the voice of God. It allows you to observe what is consistent with God's nature and what He has spoken to other spiritual men and women who have walked the earth. The Scriptures reveal a portion of the mind of God, as does the Holy Spirit. While every channel through which God speaks should be celebrated, any messages we personally receive should ultimately be weighed by the words of Scripture, to make sure we have not mistaken His voice for another.

Whenever people speak and are telling the truth, their words reveal their mind and thoughts. The Bible declares, *"God is not a man, that He should lie, nor a son of man, that He should repent; has He said, and will He not do it?"* (Numbers 23:19 NASB, NKJV). Every time God speaks a word, it reveals something of His mind.

So when I read the Bible, I don't treat it as just another book but as the disclosure of the divine mind of God.

The issue of how to judge whether a word or an impression is legitimate, as well as the Holy Spirit's role in this evaluation, will be covered later, but it is worth briefly explaining now how the Scriptures should generally be our first line of defense in such matters. For example, if someone who is already married feels "led by God" to divorce their spouse and to marry someone else because they find them attractive, that individual is not truly hearing from God. No matter how emotionally invested that person may be in the new relationship, no matter how many apparent prophetic dreams they've had "confirming" it, no matter how many supposed prophesies have been given in support of it, they can still say with confidence, "This isn't God!" Such a "leading" would be inconsistent with the teachings of the Bible. (See, for example, Matthew 5:32; Mark 10:1–12.) God's opinion concerning matrimony hasn't changed. Such a person does not have to endure either sleepless nights or days of fasting and prayer to wrestle through this question. Despite any feelings, apparent logic, or personal experiences, they are simply to dismiss the idea.

However, too many of us don't spend enough time in God's Word to establish an accurate working knowledge of His ways and to construct a proper biblical framework to guide us in the various circumstances and challenges of life. I would caution against developing a sensitivity to God's voice based on other methods of discerning divine utterance while neglecting the revealed mind and will of God found in the Bible; if you do, you will eventually drift into error, perhaps shipwrecking your faith and the faith of others.

The Holy Spirit has a vital role to play as we study God's Word or as we seek to hear God's voice through His other means of communication; and when we read the Scriptures, we must stay sensitive to His role. The job of the Holy Spirit is to take God's general, objective communication in the Bible and make it subjective or specific to our lives. In no way does this suggest that God adjusts the intent of His Word to fit our limited perspectives or desires. Rather, through His Spirit, He puts the biblical passages into a context that allows us to make personal application of them and to be transformed by them. (See, for example, Romans 12:1–2.)

For instance, with the Spirit's help, you might view the battle between David and Goliath not only as a fight between a mere youth who trusts in the mighty Jehovah and a towering warrior, but also as a story encouraging you to trust God to bring about positive cultural change through you, even though you are overshadowed by daunting societal obstacles. Through such insights from the Scriptures, we can be moved from being discouraged about our circumstances to having a confident sense of victory in our lives.

Likewise, the Holy Spirit can take one general, objective Scripture verse like *"Husbands, love your wives, just as Christ loved the church"* (Ephesians 5:25) and give it particular application for multiple individuals. For instance, if two different married men read this verse, the general interpretation would be the same in context, but the specifics of its application would probably be different for each. The context of the verse exhorts husbands to follow Christ's pattern of sacrificial love in their relationships with their wives. Husband number one reads the passage and is convicted by the Holy Spirit about the blunt and rather sarcastic way he has been speaking to his wife. Consequently, he is led by God to speak to her with consideration and gentleness. Husband number two reads the same passage and is prompted by the Holy Spirit that it wouldn't be an expression of Christlike, sacrificial love to purchase a new car for himself while his wife's vehicle remained in a broken-down condition. Each man has received a particular word from God, through the Bible, by the illumination of the Holy Spirit.

Another reason it is invaluable to read and study the Word of God is that the Holy Spirit will often bring to our mind a particular Scripture passage at exactly the time our current situation requires it, with illumination as to how its truths and principles relate to the circumstance; this can happen even when we haven't committed the verses to memory or when they're not part of our immediate recall. I consider this a subtly supernatural act on the part of the Holy Spirit, but it is supernatural nonetheless. The Spirit somehow reaches into the recesses of our mind and draws out what we would have trouble getting to on our own. This is an example of the partnership between God and human beings, and I believe it is one of the primary ways in which He speaks to us. Jesus told His disciples, *"But the Helper, the Holy Spirit, whom the Father will send in my name, He will teach you all things, and bring to your remembrance all that I said to you"* (John 14:26 NASB). Many people who lived in Palestine in Jesus' day were able to hear His teaching directly from His own mouth as He physically walked the earth with them. Today, we need to read and study the New Testament to learn what He said and taught. However, whether Jesus' words are heard or read, it is the job of the Holy Spirit to bring those words to our minds in our times of need.

THE "STILL, SMALL VOICE" OF THE HOLY SPIRIT

Another specific way God speaks to us is through the voice, or internal prompting, of the Holy Spirit. In the previous section, we discussed the Spirit's role in relation to the application of the Word to our lives. Here, we will explore His internal communications to us beyond His illumination of the Scriptures.

When we first place our faith in Christ as Savior, God not only grants us His salvation but also gives us the priceless gift of His indwelling Spirit. The Spirit literally lives within us, not as a silent partner but as an active, contributing Helper, or Advocate, who confirms our standing with God (see, for example, Romans 8:15; 2 Corinthians 1:21–22), empowers us for effective ministry (see, for example, Acts 1:8), comforts us (see John 14:26 KJV), reveals the mind of God to us (see 1 Corinthians 2:9–12), and gives us His peace (see, for example, Romans 14:17).

Many people have labeled God's communications through His Holy Spirit as His "still, small voice," after the way the Lord communicated to Elijah during a difficult time in the prophet's life. I believe that people continue to use this phrase because it describes the often subtle nature of this particular avenue of His speaking— which, though quiet, certainly does not imply a lack of power. In the following passage, note how God communicated to Elijah:

> *Then* [the Lord said] *said, "Go out, and stand on the mountain before the* LORD." *And behold, the* LORD *passed by, and a great and strong wind tore into the mountains and broke the rocks in pieces before the* LORD, *but the* LORD *was not in the wind; and after the wind an earthquake, but the* LORD *was not in the earthquake; and after the earthquake a fire, but the* LORD *was not in the fire; and after the fire **a still small voice**. So it was, when Elijah heard it, that he wrapped his face in his mantle and went out and stood in the entrance of the cave. Suddenly a voice came to him, and said, "What are you doing here, Elijah?"*   (1 Kings 19:11–13 NKJV)

Although God had at times dealt with Elijah in a powerful manner, here we find a scaled-down version of His voice. God will sometimes bring contrast or diversity to His communications in order to show that He reserves the right to speak to us in whatever manner He chooses—sometimes prominently and at other times more subtly. Whatever way He chooses, it is important for us to be able to recognize His voice and to receive His words. Those who have previously been guided by the prominent speaking of God must be extremely careful to guard against becoming desensitized to His subtle addresses.

OUR GROWTH INTO MATURITY IS NECESSARY

Because this subtle leading by God can be faint or can seem like merely a hunch or a slight prompting, it is best to pray for some form of confirmation from God to strengthen our position before we decide to take a life-altering step in relation to it. It is also important that we properly process this form of communication because, with the soft voice of the Holy Spirit, the amount of clarity we have usually depends on the level of our spiritual maturity. Jesus definitively declared, *"My sheep hear My voice"* (John 10:27 NASB, NKJV). I believe this statement contains more than just the idea of those who belong to Him being able to hear Him; the idea of maturity is implied here. After Jesus' resurrection, when He addressed Peter in order to restore the disciple to his place of ministry, He instructed him to feed both His *"sheep"* and His *"lambs,"* apparently differentiating between these two groups. (See John 21:15–17.) The term *"sheep"* indicates maturity, while *"lambs"* speaks of those who are also a part of the flock but are growing in maturity and will eventually become sheep.

These truths are key for us to remember as we learn to discern God's voice, especially in the form of His "still, small voice." As we've discovered through the account of Samuel and Eli, it's not that God isn't speaking while we are still immature in our ability to hear His voice, but simply that our ability to recognize His communications needs to be developed. Time spent in Spirit-led Bible study, in prayer (which we can define simply as communication to and from God), in uninterrupted meditation on God's Word, and in heartfelt worship helps in the maturation process. Stepping out in obedience when we feel prompted by His voice (even through trial and error) also refines our ability. In every other area of spiritual development, we give ourselves latitude to learn and to grow, so why not also in the matter of hearing God's voice through His Holy Spirit? Remember, regardless of our maturity level, we all only *"know in part"* (1 Corinthians 13:9 NASB) and need faith when being led by God's voice.

GOD SPEAKS WITH BOTH AUTHORITY AND LOVE

The Bible declares that *"the earth is the LORD's, and everything in it"* (Psalm 24:1), and that *"all authority"* belongs to Jesus (see Matthew 28:18). To help our understanding, as we learn to better recognize the internal voice of the Holy Spirit, we should realize that when He speaks, His voice is peaceful yet authoritative, because He is always in control.

My profession affords me the opportunity to interact with people from all walks of life, from leaders who govern nations to common offenders of the law. I've seen people who appear to respect nothing and no one—they terrorize their families, their communities, and anyone else who crosses their path. Loved ones, friends, and religious leaders who attempt to appeal to these seemingly unrestrained people often find their efforts futile. While there may be a plethora of factors that contribute to their outlandish dispositions, I've noticed that many of them can restrain themselves when they really want to. I've witnessed some of these same individuals in a courtroom setting, while on trial or awaiting a verdict, act completely different in their temperament or personality. They are often mannered, self-controlled, and respectful. They may dress in a suit and tie and even wear eyeglasses, whether or not they really need them. Why? Because they are standing before a judge who has the authority to determine what will happen to them for the next several years or even for the rest of their life.

Such judges rarely raise their voices or sound panicked or anxious because, in their domain, they carry full authority. Those with true authority are not intimidated, alarmed, or fearful. Consequently, if we feel any of these things in the tone of an internal utterance we receive, it probably isn't from God. There is never a time when God speaks that you ever sense weakness or lack of control; when the Master speaks there is only authority.

Furthermore, when God communicates with us internally through the Holy Spirit, He speaks to us not just with authority but also with love and grace. The Father doesn't speak condemnation over His sons and daughters. Similar to the way children will recognize when they are being disciplined by parents who truly love and care for them, we should have an overarching sense that God is pulling for us, has our best interests in mind, and loves us even while He is correcting us.

While many of us agree with this idea in principle, we often overlook it or deny it in practice. Some of us play our past mistakes over and over again in our minds, not realizing they have been forgiven and forgotten by our heavenly Father. Others falsely believe that God is telling them they must "pay" for things He's already granted them forgiveness for in Christ. For example, some women believe God has been telling them they'll never have children because they've previously had an abortion, and some men believe that their daughters will be manipulated by men because they themselves have manipulated women in the past. Thankfully, condemning voices such as these never originate from the throne of the Most High God. The Word of God says, *"Praise the LORD... who forgives all your sins and heals all your diseases, who redeems your life from the pit and crowns you with love and compassion, who satisfies your desires with good things"* (Psalm 103:2–5). Amen to that!

GOD SPEAKS THROUGH PEACE

Many people miss subtle communications from God because they are looking for prominent displays from Him, with pomp and circumstance. However, God often speaks in less dramatic ways, and one of these subtle ways is by using the presence of peace—or the lack of it—as a method of guiding us. We often experience a sense of peace when we are in His will.

A passage in Isaiah explains something of the nature of God's word (spoken or written) and its effect on its recipients: "...*so is my word that goes out from my mouth: it will not return to me empty, but will accomplish what I desire and achieve the purpose for which I sent it. You will* **go out in joy and be led forth in peace**" (Isaiah 55:11–12). Verse 11 illustrates the pinpoint accuracy of God's word in accomplishing its task, while verse 12 covers the disposition (joy) and internal position (peace) of the recipients of that word. And the New Testament states that "*the kingdom of God is...* **righteousness, peace and joy** *in the Holy Spirit*" (Romans 14:17). Taking this point further, we could say that when we are in righteous alignment to God's will, both peace and joy, made possible by the Holy Spirit, are uniquely produced in our lives. By "righteous alignment," I'm not simply speaking about the absence of sin but also about being in step with God's purpose for us in a given situation. When we begin to drift from that position or are presented with opportunities or ambitions that aren't compatible with God's will for us and we start to lean toward them, He will often speak direction or correction to us through the absence of complete peace.

What is beautifully supernatural about this method is that, many times, there is no empirical evidence to cause us concern but only the absence of peace. If we pay attention to this subtle communication, we can make vital course corrections in our lives; sometimes it is only later that we realize our making the right decision wasn't a result of our keen intellect or insight; instead, God guided us to a better place simply by removing His peace to get our attention and to show us that something wasn't right.

Let me give you an example from my own life. Before I was married, during the years when I was dating, it was my personal conviction not to allow myself to be involved in a casual relationship, which can lead to many compromises if we are not careful. My motto was, "Only date marriage material!" While my conviction didn't imply that I would marry the first woman I dated, it did provide a standard for my interactions. At any point in the courtship process, if I discovered that marriage to the young woman would not be a reality, I couldn't continue the relationship and would always courteously communicate that discovery.

I remember the last dating relationship I had before courting and marrying my wife (who was just a friend at the time). This relationship wasn't terrible or dishonoring to God by any stretch of the imagination; there were no red flags—or even yellow ones. (Yellow flags indicate the need to slow down, while red flags require that things come to a screeching halt.) In fact, every sign pointed to the possibility that things would go to the next level—engagement. The young woman I was dating possessed the qualities that were on my proverbial checklist, and from all my natural observations, she was "marriage material." She loved God, she liked me, she wanted to give her life to helping others, she knew how to have fun, she was physically attractive, and she was saving herself sexually for marriage. While no one is perfect, I couldn't find many spiritual inconsistencies in her.

Yet whenever I got close to taking the relationship to the next level, I lacked peace. Instead, it seemed as if my joy was replaced by heaviness. I didn't experience this weight in every area of my life, but only in regard to this relationship. I knew for a fact that I wasn't getting cold feet, because I desired to be married. And God didn't give me any obvious signs, Bible verses, or prophetic words to reroute my path. I believe with all my heart that God was guiding and reordering my steps in this situation by speaking to me through the avenue of His peace—in this case, the lack of it.

This form of supernatural direction communicated to me that marrying this young woman probably wasn't God's will for my life. Again, this wasn't a fleeting, one-time experience but an overarching sense every time I prepared to head down the path to engagement. It wasn't until sometime later that the incompatibility between the two of us began to surface, and we both realized that being together wasn't God's will for our lives.

While breakups are usually emotionally difficult, this one was surprisingly smooth. I found that after I'd come to the conclusion that we weren't meant to marry, my peace was immediately restored. As I mentioned earlier, during that time, my wife was simply a friend. She would call with total purity of heart to encourage me. Ironically, every time I spoke with her, I experienced complete peace and even joy. After a significant amount of time, various circumstances eventually paved the way for our marriage, which we both know was God's will for us.

I mentioned previously that there are certain things in our lives the written Word doesn't give us details about or remains neutral on—for example, which particular person to marry, whether to move from one city to another, whether to accept or turn down what seems to be a lucrative business offer, or whether to stay at one's job or launch a ministry. These are all matters the Bible does not speak to directly, and therefore God will, at times, give us specific or subjective guidance for a decision we need to make. Additionally, there are some situations in which God allows us to choose for ourselves—as we utilize good sense and wisdom. This is another aspect of our partnership with Him. But in all our decision-making, we should allow the Holy Spirit to speak to us using the presence or absence of peace as one avenue of guidance.

We should remember that the Bible's lack of specifics about the particular course of our lives has the advantage of causing us to rely fully on the Author of the Word Himself, and to come to know

Him in relationship, rather than merely having knowledge of His Word. He desires for us to read the Bible, but He wants us to get to know Him through it. It was for this reason that Jesus indicted the religious leaders of His time, saying, *"You study the Scriptures diligently because you think that in them you have eternal life. These are the very Scriptures that testify about me, yet you refuse to come to me to have life"* (John 5:39–40). Jesus wasn't minimizing the authority of Scripture but rather expressing that He wants us to have personal, interactive encounters with God. Therefore, in our daily journey, when we find ourselves in a circumstance requiring His direction and don't know whether we should proceed, if the opportunity stands up to biblical scrutiny but our best observations and prayers still leave us uncertain, we should ask ourselves, *Do I have the peace of the Holy Spirit in this?* The Scriptures tell us, *"Do not be anxious about anything, but in every situation, by prayer and petition, with thanksgiving, present your requests to God. And the peace of God, which transcends all understanding, will guard your hearts and your minds in Christ Jesus"* (Philippians 4:6–7).

11

HOW GOD SPEAKS, PART 2
DREAMS AND VISIONS, PICTURES, AND DOMINANT THOUGHTS

DREAMS AND VISIONS

Rather than begin this chapter with a statement or a contemporary story illustrating how God uses dreams and visions to communicate with us, I thought it would make more of an impact to first give some biblical examples of how He has expressed or used these methods of communication in the lives of His people:

> *Jacob left Beersheba and set out for Harran. When he reached a certain place, he stopped for the night because the sun had set. Taking one of the stones there, he put it under his head and lay down to sleep. He had a dream in which he saw a stairway resting on the earth, with its top reaching to heaven, and the angels of God were ascending and descending on it. There above it stood the LORD, and he said: "I am the LORD, the God of your father Abraham and the God of Isaac. I will give*

you and your descendants the land on which you are lying."
(Genesis 28:10–13)

In my [Ezekiel's] thirtieth year, in the fourth month on the fifth day, while I was among the exiles by the Kebar River, the heavens were opened and I saw visions of God. (Ezekiel 1:1)

In the third year of Cyrus king of Persia, a revelation was given to Daniel (who was called Belteshazzar). Its message was true and it concerned a great war. The understanding of the message came to him in a vision. (Daniel 10:1)

Because Joseph her husband was faithful to the law, and yet did not want to expose her to public disgrace, he had in mind to divorce her quietly. But after he had considered this, an angel of the Lord appeared to him in a dream and said, "Joseph son of David, do not be afraid to take Mary home as your wife, because what is conceived in her is from the Holy Spirit."
(Matthew 1:19–20)

On coming to the house, they [the Magi] saw the child with his mother Mary, and they bowed down and worshipped him. Then they opened their treasures and presented him with gifts of gold, frankincense and myrrh. And having been warned in a dream not to go back to Herod, they returned to their country by another route. When they had gone, an angel of the Lord appeared to Joseph in a dream. "Get up," he said, "take the child and his mother and escape to Egypt. Stay there until I tell you, for Herod is going to search for the child to kill him."
(Matthew 2:11–13)

About noon the following day as they were on their journey and approaching the city, Peter went up on the roof to pray. He became hungry and wanted something to eat, and while the meal was being prepared, he fell into a trance. He saw heaven opened and something like a large sheet being let down to earth by its four corners. It contained all kinds of four-footed animals, as well as reptiles and birds. Then a voice told him, "Get up, Peter. Kill and eat." "Surely not, Lord!" Peter replied. "I have never eaten anything impure or unclean." The voice spoke to him a second time, "Do not call anything impure that God has made clean." This happened three times, and immediately the sheet was taken back to heaven. (Acts 10:9–16)

One night the Lord spoke to Paul in a vision: "Do not be afraid; keep on speaking, do not be silent. For I am with you, and no one is going to attack and harm you, because I have many people in this city." (Acts 18:9–10)

These examples demonstrate that dreams and visions were legitimate, established ways by which the Lord communicated to His people in the Bible. And God still speaks through these means today:

In the last days, God says, I will pour out my Spirit on all people. Your sons and daughters will prophesy, your young men will see visions, your old men will dream dreams.
(Acts 2:17)

Since dreams and visions can be extremely similar in function and impact, I have paired the two in this section. We will begin by examining dreams.

DREAMS

One of the reasons God speaks through dreams is because when we are awake, our desires, distractions, doubts, and disbelief often occupy our attention and divert us from His purposes. The personal wiring, formation, traditions, paradigms, fears, insecurities, and limitations of our conscious mind often war against information sent to us by God. It's as if the seed of His communications is forced to grow in a field of thorns. Mature believers may wrestle less often with this issue, but to one degree or another, all of us struggle with the imposing limitations of our mental paradigms.

Sometimes this is not the result of any weakness on our part but rather is due to the magnitude attached to what God is speaking to us, which we can find difficult to take in. His plans and desires for us can be so lofty that we mentally wrestle over whether or not to believe they are possible. However, at night when we are asleep, information from God can come as a direct "download," or divine deposit, into our spirit without being blocked by any objections from our conscious mind.

Dreams are not a dominant form of communication from God to me, but lately I have experienced an unusual number of spiritually-significant dreams. Although these dreams were abstract, their meaning has unfolded, and they have helped to bring direction and clarity to my life. Based on my experiences, when a dream is from God, it tends to have distinguishing characteristics and resonates with every fiber of your being. It may take a form similar to an ordinary dream, but the sense you derive from it is often distinct, and significant events may follow the experience. Through dreams, God is able to transmit direct spiritual deposits, emotional influence, and thoughts we can actually recall long after the dream is over. For this reason, dreams are a tremendously potent form of communication from God.

A God-dream comes packaged with a sense of urgency—not necessarily with a need to carry something out, but often with a need to explore the meaning of the dream. You are rarely able to dismiss such a communication but in increasing measure give it your attention until you discover its message or implications. You realize the experience isn't ordinary, and you have a nagging suspicion there is more that God wants to reveal (if His message has not already been clarified through the dream itself).

God-dreams are also accompanied by a healthy "weight" or sense of vision. This felt weight is usually to champion, challenge, or change something. You may feel as if you have been entrusted with it, as if you're carrying an internal deposit you weren't carrying before you had the dream. The sense may be similar to what you feel after a soul-stirring spiritual encounter or Spirit-filled worship experience.

Even if a God-dream is very abstract or disorienting, you are still left with a desire to explore it further. When I have received such dreams, I have asked God for understanding, and most times it has followed immediately. It is never God's goal to confuse us, but He does desire that we request understanding. In Genesis 40, there is an account of two men who were given dreams by God. Each told his dream to Joseph, who explained their meaning after saying, *"Do not interpretations belong to God? Tell me your dreams"* (Genesis 40:8). Joseph affirmed and demonstrated that God was both the Source of their dreams and the Source of all wisdom. Likewise, when we seek God for fuller comprehension of a dream, it reconfirms to us that He is the Source of both the dream and its interpretation.

Further, when we seek to understand our God-given dreams, we place value on the revelation that has been given to us. It reveals our willingness to inconvenience ourselves to obtain an understanding of God's will, while ensuring that no "pearls" are thrown to "pigs" but rather to those who hunger and thirst and seek and knock for God's wisdom, guidance, and blessings. (See Matthew 5:6; 7:6–7; Luke 11:9.)

This is why, whenever you discern that you have been entrusted with a God-dream, it is necessary to give it priority by immediately recording it in some way (verbally or in written form) and/or seeking the Lord further about it. The proper response is never to go back to sleep with the hopes of revisiting it when you get up the next morning. Complete recall is unlikely. Moreover, you run the risk of losing a destiny-altering revelation for a mere extra hour or two of sleep.

Like prophecy, which we will explore in the next chapter, dreams don't give general guidelines or principles for living but are often personal directions or insights for an individual or a group of people. Our church experienced a communication from God in this form some months after the supernatural awakening and period of unusual miracles that I described earlier in this book. After the season of evening meetings ended, I had a dream about an almost inescapable storm brewing. The storm grew increasingly larger and fiercer. While the skies darkened, three whirlwinds became prominent, but before they could destroy everything in their path, I looked to heaven and cried out to God. An authoritative voice from heaven declared, "The only way is the shelter!" I sat up straight in my bed and asked God for clarity, and the insight He gave me was almost more than I could process.

I don't think it is necessary for me to unpack the full explanation of the dream here (that would take several chapters), but it may be fruitful to include a couple of relevant takeaways. The heart of the dream served as a spiritual forecast of sorts. The storms represented adversities we would face corporately as a church, and the dream was a prophetic snapshot that prompted us to prepare for them. Within weeks, we were struck by one adversity, temptation, or challenge after the other. If it had not been for God's message of warning through this prophetic dream, we would have been leveled without knowing what hit us; without this spiritual forecast, the storms would have descended before we were able to board the windows and take cover. Through this example, we can clearly see that there is a difference between learning godly principles from the Bible to guide our lives—as important as those are—and receiving a specific message from God that speaks to our present circumstances.

To give another example, my wife, Myesha, had a dream about her brother, for whom she had been praying for some time. She wanted God to bring desperately-needed transformation to his life, but her personal conversations and pleas with him seemed to fall on deaf ears—until God used the dream to arrest his attention. She dreamed that her brother was in a nightclub with a friend, who was hit over the head with a bottle during a fight and had to be hospitalized. She woke up and immediately called her brother. At that moment, he was in the process of getting dressed to go to a club with this very friend. After she urgently shared her dream and pleaded with him not to go, he agreed to stay home.

The next day, she learned the impact of this dream. Her brother stopped by our house, visibly shaken. When she asked what was going on, he told her that his friend had gone to the club the night before and a fight had broken out. Not only that, but he had been hit over the head with a bottle and required medical attention.

My wife might have dismissed the word from God as a foolish notion if it had come in the form of a fleeting thought, but the dream had come to her in such a compelling manner that she had felt the need to respond immediately by calling her brother, and I'm glad she did! Her brother discovered the reality of God's love and protection, and he hasn't been the same since!

VISIONS

A God-given dream is a scene (or scenes) with significant meaning given while we are asleep, whereas a God-given vision is a scene (or scenes) that come into our minds or even into our sight while we are awake. In the Bible, we find examples of visions that varied in scale in terms of display and impact. The apostle Paul was leveled by a vision of the resurrected Christ, but he also received at least one vision that was subtler in nature. (See, for example, Acts 9:1–18; Acts 16:9–10.) My focus in this section isn't on visions that are overwhelmingly compelling and prominent. I don't think most people would have difficulty recognizing such experiences as communications from God. Instead, my primary goal is to explain the nature of the smaller, more subtle visions, which occur more frequently.

A vision often feels like a daydream, but it has the same feeling of urgency or significance that is attached to a God-dream. For example, during my first years of ministry, when I was in my late teens/early twenties, I went to the movies one evening with my father and my brother Chris. While we were standing in line for tickets, a young woman approached me and said hello. She followed up with, "What are you going to see?" I told her the title of the film, and to my surprise she pulled out two tickets to the same movie and asked if I wanted to go with her. I immediately declined her offer, telling her I was with my family. However, my reason for declining wasn't only the desire for quality family time but also a concern for my religious image and reputation. It didn't help that this young woman was wearing the shortest dress I've ever seen anyone wear in public. If one of the deacons or church mothers had seen me out with her, I never would have recovered from the cloud of suspicion that would have created (or so I thought at the time).

After I turned down her offer, she hung her head and disappeared into the night crowd. We got our tickets and made our way to the concession stand, where a slight sense of conviction began to come over me. I had dismissed this lonely girl as if she were an annoying salesman with a gimmick. I hadn't even dignified her request with a kind rejection. This happened during the height of the "WWJD" wristband movement. Feeling bad about my actions, the question "What would Jesus do?" permeated my mind. But I thought, *Oh well; it's too late; she's already gone.* I found comfort in the fact that I would do better if the opportunity presented itself again—but at the same time, I felt relieved that I didn't have to deal with it right then.

Not thirty seconds later, my brother elbowed me and pointed to the young woman, who had once again emerged behind me in line. With my newfound revelation, I turned to her, still with a great deal of hesitancy, and asked through closed teeth, "Would you like to sit with me and my family?" Her countenance brightened, her smile beamed, and after almost leaping, she composed herself and said, "Sure!"

About thirty minutes into the movie, I became distracted by something that seemed like daydreams, but they appeared to have significance. I began to see moving images of men having their way with this girl (in the form of silhouettes) and literally taking advantage of her by violating her sexually. This experience started with just a fleeting image, but the urgency attached to it became more pronounced with every moment that passed. I soon realized that these weren't random thoughts but insights from God. Obviously, He hadn't given me access to this information in order to make me feel spiritual or to cause me to distance myself from this young woman, but to minister to her.

My challenge now was one of appropriateness. How does one address something so intimate in a public theater? As I deliberated about this, time went by, and my window of opportunity narrowed. The movie was about to end, and I was still deliberating about what to do. In my anxiety, I offered a plea to God for help, and the Holy Spirit, the ultimate Helper, spoke to me in my time of need by bringing to mind a biblical passage I had previously studied. He reminded me of Jesus' interaction with the Samaritan woman at the well, recorded in John 4. The specific point the Holy Spirit highlighted for me was how Jesus had addressed the woman with the supernaturally perceived information He had received from the Father concerning her. Jesus didn't *ask* her about the details of her life, but rather *told* her those details. (See John 4:16–17.)

I realized that the Lord didn't want me to be tentative when I talked with the young woman about the vision I'd received but to be direct about it. I fought my natural inclination to ask her if she had been taken advantage of and instead turned to her while she was still enjoying the movie and stated, "You've been taken advantage of." She looked at me with shock on her face; then tears immediately began to flow from her eyes.

I shared with her a bit more about what the Lord had revealed to me through the vision, and she slowly dipped her head in shame. But before she could sink into discouragement, I told her, "God didn't show that to me to discourage you but to let you know that you are still on His mind and that He loves you more than you can imagine." I prayed with her and continued to encourage her, and we eventually parted. I don't know how the conversations went when she was back with her family and friends, but I would like to think she made mention of a Jesus-loving, divinely-inspired man who "told her everything she had done." (See John 4:28–29.) In that situation, it was amazing to see the hope and encouragement of our heavenly Father being released as a result of a simple vision.

To conclude this section about God-given dreams and visions, let me emphasize that we have a great responsibility to properly handle them. There is nothing spiritual about giving confusing information to people or presenting it in an inappropriate way. We can either draw people to God or cause them to be repelled from Him and from us if these special communications from Him are not handled correctly.

Dreams and visions often defy the rules of space, time, and chronological order. We shouldn't look for them to be completely logical to us before we recognize them as coming from God; they can come illogically packaged. It is the interpretation that is logical and makes them significant. Before expressing a dream or a vision that you've received as a message for another person, make sure you pray for understanding. You might also discuss it beforehand with a more experienced believer for help with the interpretation. Then seek the Holy Spirit for the best way to present the information. Again, a lack of clarity from you will simply promote disorientation in others. I suspect that this is one of the main reasons people are so apprehensive about the idea of God speaking through dreams and visions. So please handle them responsibly!

PICTURES

God-given pictures are similar to visions in that they take place while we are awake and can have the same spiritual sense or impact carried by dreams and visions. However, instead of being moving scenes, they tend to be revelations in the form of fleeting, still images or snapshots that carry meaning. For example, during your devotional time while you are praying, or even at another time, someone's face may flash across your mind. When this happens to me, I first ask the Father if there is a specific message or word for that person. Whether I receive one or not, I give the person a call, and even with that I have experienced some amazing results. Often, the people whose faces have flashed across my mind are in need of encouragement or even deeper ministry. As I mentioned in a previous chapter, after having received such promptings, I have been used by God to prevent people who were about to engage in extramarital affairs or who were on their way to commit suicide from carrying out their intentions.

Moreover, while you are praying for someone in person at church, at home, or anywhere else, as you stay sensitive to the ways the Lord speaks through you, He may give you a picture that will unlock prophetic insights and heighten the ministry encounter. I wrote earlier about how one such "snapshot" of my mother with grey hair changed her life after it was shared with her, because she had been oppressed by the thought of dying young. Pictures are usually given by God when there is a need to convey profound truth in a limited or concise timeframe, or when the subject of our ministry has a short attention span and needs to receive a communication from God that will make a strong and immediate impact. The phrase "a picture is worth a thousand words" couldn't be truer than in this context.

God's divine images are concise but also complex, just like physical snapshots or pictures. Often, the more you observe a picture, the more you observe about it. So while there is usually only one God-given picture, multiple revelations can be drawn from it.

When I am speaking to a live audience, I like to use a simple exercise to give people a sense of what it is like to receive a divine picture. I ask those present to try their best to clear their minds of distractions but to stay alert, with their eyes open. Then I say words that were familiar to millions of children who were learning to read in the second half of the twentieth century. I simply utter the three words, "See Spot run." Then I ask the question, "What did you see?" While awake and aware—this is a completely natural process; no one goes into a "trance" or has "convulsions"—everyone gets an image of some sort. When questioned about their experience, some say they recalled the drawing of the little dog from their primary school book, some say they pictured a real dog in stride, some say they imagined a "spot" bouncing, and others say they saw the words "See Spot run" in sentence form. The point is that each person saw some mental picture that could be clearly articulated.

This is very similar to the way God speaks through pictures. He will give a snapshot or a mental picture, often with meaning attached, while you are engaged in the everyday activities of life. It could happen during your devotions, but it could also occur while you are in a business meeting, at the movies, or worshipping at church. There is no setting where these miraculous snapshots are off-limits.

DOMINANT THOUGHTS

A God-given dominant thought is similar to a picture or a vision in its prominence, weightiness, and impact; however, it doesn't surface as an image but rather as a notion or an idea. If you've ever been in the market for a car and become absorbed in the process of comparing makes, models, specifications, and prices, then you already have an understanding of this concept in a natural sense. While you still have to go about your daily life—working, making and eating meals, engaging in conversations, and interacting with people in other ways, you are a bit preoccupied or consumed with the dominant thought of finding "the" right car. Until the deal is done, and even afterwards, what reverberates most in your mind are the thoughts about that vehicle. Similarly, when God speaks through a dominant thought, He causes one truth, phrase, concept, or word to permeate your mind or resonate more than any others.

A dominant thought from God might also be described as a spiritually significant "eureka" moment. The thought or idea that is downloaded from heaven is usually beyond what we would come up with through natural observation or contemplation; or we arrive at a conclusion without the mental deliberation it would normally take to get there. You know you've had a dominant thought when you've completely grasped C without ever having been aware of A and B.

In the next chapter, we will explore three additional ways in which God speaks to us, and then we will look more closely at how to discern whether a communication we receive is truly from God.

12

HOW GOD SPEAKS, PART 3
EQUIPPING MINISTERS, PROPHETIC WORDS, AND OPEN AND CLOSED DOORS

GOD'S EQUIPPING MINISTERS

> So Christ himself gave the apostles, the prophets, the evange-
> lists, the pastors and teachers, to equip his people for works
> of service, so that the body of Christ may be built up until we
> all reach unity in the faith and in the knowledge of the Son of
> God and become mature, attaining to the whole measure of the
> fullness of Christ.   (Ephesians 4:11–13)

While all of us who place our faith in Jesus Christ are ministers
of His gospel, we each have different roles to play. The above passage indicates that God uses two types of believers to accomplish
His work on earth: those whose main task is to *equip*—apostles,
prophets, evangelists, pastors, and teachers—and those whose
main task is to execute or do the *works of service.* Of course,
everyone is called to execute something on God's behalf, but some

people's emphasis is more on the spiritual formation of others than on the implementation of the work or service itself. For the purposes of this book, I have chosen to call these believers "Equipping Ministers."

While the dispositions, assignments, vantage points, and modes of expression used by the Equipping Ministers may differ, the medium they use to build up others is usually the same—verbal expression (even though the whole of their lives and character is a witness). This form of verbal expression is one more example of how God desires to reveal His purposes and plans to His people.

Specifically, God often uses these ministers to deliver His insights, direction, and equipping in a Christian community setting. When these ministers speak, they may have personal benefits or insights for individuals, but their primary contribution is usually to a corporate body of believers. Their role becomes essential when you consider how chaotic it would be to try to advance a group of individuals who all have their own wills, agendas, spiritual biases, scriptural interpretations, and maturity levels. The task of such ministers is to build, to compel, to care for, to declare, and to instruct people in a way that provides clarity concerning the task before them, promotes unity, and produces maturity in all.

There was no such thing in the first-century church as a believer who was independent of the rest of the body of believers. In the corporate setting, while everyone had the ability to personally commune with God and to contribute to the local spiritual gatherings, there were always voices of clarity, direction, insight, and godly authority that emerged amid the others. In the context of healthy gatherings, these voices came with a greater degree of weight than the others; they were the voices of the apostle, the prophet, the evangelist, the pastor, and the teacher.

I want to be crystal clear about what I am saying in order to avoid abuses of this principle. As previously stated, every utterance that is alleged to be from God must be weighed, including words from ministers of the gospel. We should not think that everything that comes from our spiritual leaders is to be received as divine or that they are less flawed than any of God's other vessels. But their words are to be respected, listened to, and weighed according to scriptural guidelines.

Although social trends, philosophical frameworks, and scientific theories have changed over the last couple of millennia, I believe God's intent to equip His people by His words through His Equipping Ministers remains the same. It is still one of the primary ways He speaks to His people corporately. This is one reason it is vital for every Christian to be connected to a local body of believers. Without a doubt, God can speak to us individually, when we are by ourselves, but the words He speaks to us in private are often magnified or put into proper context when considered in light of what He is saying to the corporate body. The spiritual community you are a part of and the words of the ministers of that body should play a significant role in your spiritual life (given that the environment is a healthy one). So, again, the voices of the Equipping Ministers should be received with a degree of weight and prominence, and with a reasonable amount of authority:

> Have confidence in your leaders and submit to their authority, because they keep watch over you as those who must give an account. (Hebrews 13:17)

If you are in a place where your heart cannot rest with a spiritual leader and you're experiencing more skepticism than trust, it is probably time for you to prayerfully consider a transition to a different community of believers. In the ideal scenario, a leader's words should challenge, convict, inspire, confirm, develop, reveal, or prepare you for something God is doing or for the plans He has for you and the other believers you're connected to. Remember, He will not speak through only one individual to you, because then you might not seek Him personally; neither will He always speak directly to you, because then you might neglect the beauty of living in community with other believers. Therefore, there is a dimension of God's will for your life that will never be disclosed until you learn to hear and receive what He speaks to you through others.

PROPHETIC WORDS

> *Follow the way of love and eagerly desire gifts of the Spirit, especially prophecy.... What then shall we say, brothers and sisters? When you come together, each of you has a hymn, or a word of instruction, a revelation, a tongue or an interpretation. Everything must be done so that the church may be built up.... Two or three prophets should speak, and the others should weigh carefully what is said. And if a revelation comes to someone who is sitting down, the first speaker should stop. For you can all prophesy in turn so that everyone may be instructed and encouraged. The spirits of prophets are subject to the control of prophets. For God is not a God of disorder but of peace—as in all the congregations of the Lord's people.*
>
> (1 Corinthians 14:1, 26, 29–33)

The gift of prophecy is misunderstood by many in the church, causing some people to fear it and others to dismiss it altogether. Many people don't esteem the prophetic ministry because it is prone to abuses, often at the hands of manipulative or outright "weird" messengers. Prophecy, however, should not be shunned but rather celebrated as a means through which God communicates to us. In fact, Paul taught Christians in the early church, *"Do not quench the Spirit; do not despise prophetic utterances"* (1 Thessalonians 5:19–20 NASB). This passage encourages us not to throw a wet blanket over the Spirit's flame in the context of this corporate (or even personal) ministry. It is implied through the sacred text that this is what happens when we forbid, shun, or discourage prophecy.

The body of Christ does itself a disservice whenever we celebrate and employ the other spiritual gifts but neglect the prophetic one. While it is true that the gift or ministry of prophesy can be abused, the reality is that there are abuses and misappropriations with every gift. If we thought about it, we would quickly realize that we probably have, on average, more abuses and error associated with the gift of teaching than we do with the gift of prophecy. However, we don't throw the entire gift of teaching and its practice under the bus because of the people who misuse them.

Others steer clear of prophecy due to ignorance about the nature of this gift. As I mentioned in a previous chapter, the Bible clearly says, *"We know in part and we prophesy in part"* (1 Corinthians 13:9 NASB). One application of this is that the vessels whom God is using don't always have the full picture but must often employ their faith and interpretive ability before sharing a word they believe is from God. While those who hear a prophecy must carefully examine it, as well as the spirit of the person who is prophesying, there is no such thing as 100 percent accuracy, 100 percent of the time, from 100 percent of those who prophesy, especially among those who are learning to grow in the gift. If that or anything close to it is your expectation, you will never be able to benefit from this method through which God speaks to us. The greatest prophetic voices still see only bits and pieces of the picture but usually have enough of it to, by faith, articulate a meaningful message.[5]

First Thessalonians 5 further reveals the nature of our interaction with prophecy by saying, *"Examine everything carefully; hold fast to that which is good"* (verse 21 NASB). Some prophesies are to be rejected

---

5. For more on the nature of prophesy and testing prophecy, see Derek Prince, *The Gifts of the Spirit* (New Kensington, PA: Whitaker House, 2007), chapters 11 and 12.

as erroneous, but other prophecies aren't to be abandoned altogether for having small interpretive errors, or where there isn't 100 percent accuracy. There is a big difference between actual false prophets—who have deceitful intent or have allowed themselves to come under demonic influence (see, for example, Matthew 7:15–16; 1 John 4:1)—and those who receive a prophetic word or other revelation and make an unwitting error or allow pride or another wrong attitude to distort the communication. Paul gave us the latitude to hold on to what was good, valuable, and completely accurate about a prophecy without rejecting everything in it because of a lack of clarity or a misrepresentation in one area.

The nature of the prophetic in our day is not to receive a message or revelation from God that is perfection and will later be canonized in Scripture; rather, prophecy is given to build up the body of Christ and to prompt people toward the purposes of God for their lives. *"But the one who prophesies speaks to people for their strengthening, encouraging and comfort"* (1 Corinthians 14:3).

Let me give you another example from my days as a single man. My girlfriend, Myesha, and I had broken up, and I was not involved in any relationship whatsoever. A friend of mine came with a team from Wellington, New Zealand, to minister at our church on a Sunday. After he finished his message, he asked his team to pray with people and share a personal word of prophecy—if the Lord gave them one. A lady walked up to me and said several accurate things concerning my personal life and ministry, as revealed by the Lord, and I received it all gladly. However, when she got to the end of her prophesy, she spoke something that raised a red flag in my mind. She ended her time of ministry with the statement, "God is restoring the relationship with your wife…. Amen!" While I received most of what she said, the problem was that I wasn't married and had no wife to be restored to. I now had a choice to make. Should I reject every word she uttered, or should I "hold fast to" the accurate while dismissing the inaccurate? I chose the latter because I understood the nature of prophecy in the church and that "we all know in part and prophesy in part." We are often forced to express what we feel we are receiving from God over small chasms and interpretive blind spots.

Interestingly, not long after that prophecy, my relationship with Myesha was restored, and she later became my wife. It wasn't that the words of the woman on the ministry team had been inaccurate; it was simply that she had received a picture or revelation of marriage and the restoration of my relationship but had to interpret what she saw "in part" and find the language in her limited understanding to communicate God's message to me.

As I mentioned earlier in relation to other forms of communication from God, the Lord often leaves what I call divine blind spots. He will not reveal everything we need to know in our personal encounters with Him, nor will He supply everything we need through our encounters with other people. If He were to reveal everything to us directly, we might start to think we were able to act independent of people—or we might focus exclusively on Him and disregard the necessary relationships and gifts He has deposited in His church through the members of the body. Similarly, if the Lord gave 100 percent disclosure to any one minister of His church, that minister might become our primary source, and we would likely neglect our intimate relationship with God. Consequently, He intentionally leaves blind spots in these two areas to highlight our need for both.

I often hear people say, "If God has a message for me, He can give it to me directly!" Again, that would fulfill the role of revelation but would downplay the avenue of God speaking through others, which not only provides revelation but also promotes unity and community. Whenever God speaks to us through someone else in a miraculous manner, disclosing our innermost thoughts or circumstances, we should be drawn again to God in amazement and carry a greater appreciation for the vessel He used to communicate His message.

Finally, let me say that with regard to your receiving prophetic words for others, such communications may come in the form of a dream, a vision, a picture, an insight while reading Scripture, or any of the other ways in which God speaks. The only difference is that the final recipient of the word is not yourself but someone else. Like dreams and visions, prophetic words can sometimes be a bit abstract. When this is the case, ask God for insight and perhaps consult with a more experienced believer about the interpretation before passing along a word. You can also explain it to the recipient as best you can and ask if it means anything to them. Never assume that the weirder the presentation, the more spiritual it is. Remember, when Jesus spoke in abstract or confusing symbolism, it was often to cloak His message from those who had wrong motives or impure hearts. When He spoke to His disciples, He always provided them with clear understanding. We must learn to make God's communications clear enough for Him to be glorified as His people are edified. So if you ever receive a word from God that you feel is for another person, please remember that the goal is always to promote clarity and never to create confusion.

OPEN AND CLOSED DOORS

> *Paul and his companions traveled throughout the region of Phrygia and Galatia, having been kept by the Holy Spirit from preaching the word in the province of Asia. When they came to the border of Mysia, they tried to enter Bithynia, but* **the Spirit of Jesus would not allow them to.** *So they passed by Mysia and went down to Troas.*   (Acts 16:6–8)

This passage reveals one more way in which God speaks to us—through open and closed doors. A fairly common challenge among believers who desire to be led by God is the issue of paralysis due to uncertainty. There are times when we take a posture of inactivity, not wanting to move forward with plans, desires, ministry initiatives, or goals until we get a clear and compelling personal directive from the Lord. Interestingly, in the above account, we find that Paul and his ministry companions had already started on their way to Asia (among other places) on a missionary journey when they were prevented by the Holy Spirit from going to that region. Paul had not passively waited for specific directives but rather had been proactive in response to the general directive from God that he had been given, until he was prevented by the Spirit from carrying out some of his particular plans. The general directive for followers of Jesus was, "*Go into all the world and preach the gospel to all creation*" (Mark 16:15). Within this directive, a major focus of Paul's role as an apostle was "*to proclaim* [Jesus'] *name to the Gentiles and their kings…*" (Acts 9:15), which he had been attempting to do.

There are several reasons why God may choose to guide us using open and closed doors. Sometimes, as with the avenue of dreams, He does so because His scope for our life's purpose is much larger than our own; it is beyond what we think we're capable of pursuing. Consequently, He reserves the right to interrupt our plans in order to align us with His divine purpose. In some instances, He is forced to close doors of apparent opportunity because our intense desire for something that is not in sync with His plans has caused us to push past the common indicators of divine guidance, such as promptings, revelation, lack of peace, and red flags. A closed door of opportunity in our lives has the ability to capture our attention in a way that some of the other, more subtle, communications from the Lord might not. There are times when I am uncertain about which direction God is leading me, and I debate internally about what my next steps should be. However, over the years, I've learned that sometimes God reveals His will and guides me by overriding my desires with closed doors.

While God may close doors in order to redirect our steps, He may also open doors of opportunity in unlikely places and at unusual times for the purpose of guiding us into what He has in store for us. The passage in Acts 16 continues with an account of God leading Paul to Macedonia through a vision in the night:

> *During the night Paul had a vision of a man of Macedonia standing and begging him, "Come over to Macedonia and help us." After Paul had seen the vision, we got ready at once to leave for Macedonia, concluding that God had called us to preach the gospel to them.*   (Acts 16:9–10)

Macedonia, a place of great need, was primed for Paul's unique ministry style and skill set. It wasn't the place he would have chosen, but thank God he was spiritually sensitive enough to know that God speaks through open and closed doors and visions. In fact, I believe a closed door or frustrated opportunity usually precedes our entry into a greater, more purposeful opening from God. So instead of stewing in frustration the next time a door of opportunity closes, learn to ask the Lord, "Are You speaking? What would You have me do next?"

13

CONFIRMING COMMUNICATIONS FROM GOD

As a way to briefly review the last three chapters, and for further clarification on what we've discussed, let us explore an important issue that often arises concerning our understanding of the still, small voice of the Lord and sometimes even His more prominent communications. This issue is not an inability to hear but rather an uncertainty about the origin of a word or another communication we receive. In this situation, we ask ourselves, *Was that really God, or was that me?* Or even, *Was that the devil?*

I understand this confusion because when God speaks in a subtle manner, it can sometimes be hard for us to distinguish it from self-talk or even from thoughts of temptation. Generally, when God speaks or plants a thought or an idea in your mind, your internal voice doesn't change its tone to sound like the deep resonance of actor James Earl Jones or that of a radio announcer. Instead, as in other instances of communication from God, you may feel a sense of urgency, divine deposit, or healthy burden. But again, because such thoughts can seem like our own, I think it's important for us to use some spiritual tests to help identify the origin of an utterance or any other communication, especially one that can have a significant impact on our lives.

Additionally, we are bombarded with so much information, emotional manipulation, and solicitation from the culture around us that it is essential to be able to retain the thoughts and ideas that we need while disregarding what we don't. As Paul wrote, we are to think about *"whatever is true, whatever is noble, whatever is right, whatever is pure, whatever is lovely, whatever is admirable"* (Philippians 4:8).

Like a water purification system or a gold-mining sifter, a spiritual filtering process is useful for discerning the true voice of the Lord and also for determining what thoughts are healthy to retain. I've noticed that in a physical filtration process or sifting method, the procedure always starts broad, allowing the larger items of debris to pass through, and then narrows, straining more intensely at the smaller pieces with subsequent phases of the movement. This straining takes place until the recipient is left with exactly what is desired.

In the spiritual life, we're not after gold or purified water but rather the riches of what God is saying to us and the life-giving water of His Word. So in order for our spiritual filtration process to yield what we desire, we, too, must start broad and narrow the filter until we are left with only God's precious words and will.

The filter we use to discover the genuine voice of God has four "straining stations." As we have seen, two of them also function as means of spiritual communication. They are, from broadest to narrowest: (1) the Bible, (2) the character of God, (3) the Holy Spirit, and (4) the glorification test. The combination of these four indicators allows us to confirm that a word or other communication is genuinely from God. Their order does not indicate descending prominence or importance but rather the process by which we are able to narrow and affirm (or disaffirm) any words we receive.

1. *The Bible.* When I first hear an internal word or feel an inner prompting and want to know whether it's from God and should

be acted upon, I ask, "How does what I'm hearing line up with a biblical framework?" As our standard for soundness, the Bible is our most general filter. If what is being suggested to me violates the revealed will of God through Scripture, I immediately dismiss it as not having its origins in God. Any suggestion that goes against the basic teaching of Scripture should be ignored, such as the idea of divorcing your spouse simply because you find someone else "more attractive." Similarly, if you feel the Lord is "telling you" to get drunk in order to take the focus off your problems and enjoy Him better, you can be assured that word is not from Him. The Scriptures say, *"Do not get drunk on wine, which leads to debauchery* [in other words, it will ruin your life]. *Instead, be filled with the Spirit"* (Ephesians 5:18). That word about getting drunk will clearly be caught by the filter of Scripture so that you won't even need to take it to the next level of processing.

2. *The Character of God.* The second filter, which is even narrower in its scrutiny, is the character of God. In Luke 4, the Bible records the temptation of Jesus by the devil. While I won't unpack this encounter in its entirety, I do want to point out one interesting fact. In verses 3–11, the devil tempted Jesus three times, but he saved his trickiest temptation for last: Satan used an actual Bible passage in his attempt to deceive Jesus:

> *The devil led him to Jerusalem and had him stand on the highest point of the temple. "If you are the Son of God," he said, "throw yourself down from here. For it is written: 'He will command his angels concerning you to guard you carefully; they will lift you up in their hands, so that you will not strike your foot against a stone.' Jesus answered, "It is said: 'Do not put the Lord your God to the test.'"* (Luke 4:9–12)

The devil tried to get Jesus to make the wilderness experience about Himself by putting God to the test, and he used words found in Psalm 91:11–12 to do it. This account proves that we need an even narrower test or filter when words from the Bible are used to prompt us to a particular action. The mishandling or manipulation of the words of Scripture is rampant in our day and can be a devastating tool of unscrupulous people. Even a wrong emphasis on portions of Scripture—intentional or not—can lead people into error. What allowed Jesus to reject the word of the enemy, even when he quoted Scripture, was the fact that He thoroughly knew the character of His heavenly Father and therefore was quickly able to distinguish which ideas and suggestions were consistent with that character and which were not. What allowed Him to refute the solicitation of the devil, while revealing the true intent of God by responding with another Scripture, was His intimate affiliation with the Father. Jesus' Scripture trumped the Scripture used by the devil, even though all the words were biblical. It's as if Jesus was saying, "You've read the Book, but I know the Author," or "Applying that Scripture in this way doesn't match the character of the Author!"

Though Satan's temptation might have made it through the Bible filter, it did not make it through the character of God filter, which helps us to keep Scripture in the spirit it was intended to be received in. A knowledge of God's character comes from quality, uninterrupted time spent with Him, and from observing His broad dealings and behaviors with human beings as demonstrated through the entire tenor of Scripture.

3. *The Holy Spirit.* In our world, there is much solicitation to inappropriate or unfruitful activity that won't necessarily be sifted out by an obvious Scripture passage or be found to be in conflict with the character of God. When a word comes to us and does not violate the Bible or what we know of the character of God, there is an even finer Sifter available to us in the person of the indwelling Holy Spirit. Again, the Spirit doesn't guide us only by biblical

principles we've studied or by Scripture we've memorized but also by giving us access to the mind of God. He adds a miraculous dimension to our minds that is beyond our physical observations or study. Paul wrote, *"The Spirit searches all things, even the deep things of God"* (1 Corinthians 2:10). This truth is vital because, if you have studied philosophy, you'll know that at the deepest levels of logic, ungodly and even evil things can appear rational to people if they are presented in the right way or if they are buried under enough subterfuge. The human mind is not always clever enough to catch it all, but the Holy Spirit is not bound by the confines of human limitation and can cut through the deception.

Years ago, a woman in her late fifties, accompanied by two young women, began coming to our church. They attended almost every service, lifted their hands as we worshipped, went to Bible studies regularly, and contributed fitting input when called upon in small groups. One day, one of the young ladies approached me with a proposed study she wanted to teach, and later explained it was what God had told her to share with me. As I processed her request in the days that followed, I received what I believed to be a divine word of guidance about it, and it was "No!" It wasn't that she was asking something that was unbiblical or violated the character of God; it just didn't make it past the Holy Spirit sifter. Rather than creating rest in my spirit, the request actually unsettled me the more I thought about it. When I gave the young woman my answer, she became upset, and all three women left the church, never to be seen again.

A few weeks later, I received a call from a colleague in my city who was familiar with these ladies and had heard they were attending our ministry. He told me that they had been to his church and had caused tremendous devastation. Then he gave me convincing proofs that these women were actually witches and that their modus operandi was to work their way into the fabric of local churches to eventually create discord, confusion, and false accusations. There would have been no observable clues until it was too late. Thankfully, the Holy Spirit catches and filters what we tend to miss!

4. *The Glorification Test.* If there is ever any doubt concerning the origin of a word after you've used the filters of the Bible, God's character, and the Holy Spirit, one final filter may be considered—the "glory" filter. With this test, we ask ourselves the simple question, *Who will get the glory from my response to this word or prompting that I sense?* I've found that the devil won't encourage you to do what glorifies God; your selfish ambition is preoccupied with glory for itself, while God leads you in pursuits that honor Him. As David wrote, *"He leads me in the paths of righteousness for His name's sake"* (Psalm 23:3 NKJV).

PART THREE: RESPONDING

14

DOING THE WILL

In parts one and two, we explored the importance of hearing the voice of the Lord and how we can tune our hearts in a manner that will allow us to recognize when He is speaking. But the process won't be complete until we step out and respond to what our heavenly Father says. The chapters that follow were written to help you respond to God's direction with intention, courage, and immediacy, so that you can begin to fulfill your miraculous potential.

CONFORMED TO THE IMAGE OF JESUS

What is our ultimate aim as we seek to listen to the Father and respond to Him? It is to become conformed to the image of Jesus and to model our relationship with God based on His interactions with the Father in every area of our lives. Most believers would agree that the clear standard for our relationship with God the Father, in thought and behavioral pattern, is the life Jesus modeled for us while physically on earth. His words and deeds create the perfect standard for righteousness and for our functioning in divine power and love. As devoted followers of Jesus, our goal is to be imitators of Him.

However, many people attempt to pattern themselves after Christ merely by observing His lifestyle, His words, and His responses, and then trying to mold their behavior to fit them. While a character study of the life of Christ is a significant first step in familiarizing ourselves with His ways, His actions weren't manifested to be observed and mechanically repeated but to cause us to draw nearer to the Source (God) of those actions. Following Jesus is not simply a matter of behavior modification. As we have seen, to be conformed to the life of Jesus, we must understand and develop the same "internal driver" that He had—the same responsiveness that enabled Him to clearly hear and wholeheartedly obey the will of the Father. We can't be imitators of Jesus without adopting the internal engine that produced His behavior—which was an ability to maintain communion with the Father, hear His voice, and respond to it.

As we do this, we learn to receive direct promptings from the Father that will produce organic behavioral patterns consistent with those of His Son. As Jesus said, *"Truly, truly, I say to you, the Son can do nothing of Himself, unless it is something He sees the Father doing; for whatever the Father does, these things the Son also does in like manner"* (John 5:19 NASB).

So again, our imitation of Christ is not just a surface-level repetition of His actions, captured through reading the biblical accounts, but also an adoption of the internal engine that allowed Him to produce those actions. Thus, our ultimate goal is never simply to observe and repeat but *to commune and manifest.* The "observe and repeat" phase of our faith journey is intended to be the training wheels to get us to the "hear and do" stage of relational maturity, interaction, and expression. I believe with all my heart that this is what it means to be an *imitator* of Christ in the fullest sense of the word. Anything else would be settling for an inferior spiritual position—a mere religious form without the underlying divine communion. Jesus' behavior was always a product of His intimacy with God, and He modeled this way of life for us, inviting us to follow Him into it.

We cannot hope to experience the miraculous life with any level of consistency without becoming a true imitator of Jesus in this way. It is God's task to speak, it is our task to respond, and it is His task to produce the miraculous. We often spend too much time being concerned with how He will perform His tasks and not enough on performing our own portion of the equation. When we learn to properly respond, He will produce results through our lives that are beyond our comprehension. Some results of His speaking will be more pronounced and dramatic than others, but they should all be celebrated as divinely inspired or miraculously empowered. That is why, when we overcome the limitations that keep us from responding to the divine utterances of God, our lives will become testimonies of His presence and power.

POWER WITHOUT ACCESS

Just as we need to overcome various hindrances in our ability to hear the voice of God, we need to remove the barriers that prevent us from responding once we've heard His voice. Having the ability to hear without the capacity or willingness to respond is like owning a home that is wired for electricity but lacks the proper electrical outlets to access it. The power is present but can never be utilized. As believers, we are the conduits through which much of God's power is expressed and manifested to others. Therefore, the factors that affect our reaction to His revelation and our willingness to express His words and works are significant issues. We must discover the obstacles that stand in the way of our bold response to God's will and words—and, then, how to remove them.

Remember that God works in tandem with men and women to accomplish His purposes on earth. This reality presents humanity with both a blessing and a challenge. The blessing is that the God of all creation would choose to use His created ones as His divine instruments. There is no greater honor than this calling, and that thought alone should produce an overwhelming sense of gratitude in us. However, the challenge associated with God choosing to work through us is that we can delay, partially obey, distort, and even ignore His promptings. Consequently, the results are short-circuited—or never even realized—and both we and the other intended recipients of God's blessings are inevitably affected. The good news is that God is extremely patient, doesn't give up on us, and is constantly at work within us to encourage our obedience. (See, for example, Philippians 2:13.)

Let's look at some examples of this. The Bible reveals that while God, in His omnipotence, can produce instantaneous results or deliverance, He has often sovereignly chosen to work some of His almighty power through His people. For instance, when the Israelites were under the bonds of slavery in Egypt, God could have freed them Himself, but instead He chose the uncertain and insecure Moses to lead them out. (See, for example, Exodus 3.) Later, when the Midianite army was terrorizing Israel, He could have removed His people's enemies by Himself, but instead He worked through the fearful Gideon. (See Judges 6.) When it came to electing a messenger to warn the Ninevite people to repent, God didn't choose a willing prophet but a partially-prejudiced one named Jonah. (See Jonah 1–4.) Interestingly, God didn't take a by-any-means-necessary approach to accomplishing His will. He didn't simply move on without these leaders due to their initial reluctance; He didn't immediately look for a substitute or take care of things on His own. He helped these leaders through their usability issues and hang-ups and produced miraculous results through each of their lives, for His purposes and glory.

GRACE IN OUR WEAKNESS

I am convinced that the God of the Bible doesn't want to abandon us, either, in the midst of our limitations, weaknesses, hesitation, or procrastination, but still desires to use us to accomplish His purposes. For us, it is a matter of getting past the barriers to responding to His will so we can move forward in the miraculous life.

When God directs His people to do something, He speaks from a limitless reality (eternity) into the context of a limited reality (our lives on earth). It is no wonder that we have to undergo a process of learning to hear and respond to Him! Even as people of faith, we are riddled with fears, failures, distractions, doubts, disappointments, insecurities, uncertainties, ignorance, and pain in our lives and circumstances. Yet we are the very instruments God has chosen to bring His miraculous power to bear on those issues in our lives and in the lives of others. Before we can respond to His instructions, however, we must fortify certain areas of our lives while dismantling the barriers that hinder us. Again, the good news is that we have a God who specializes in the redemption and empowerment process and can shatter the walls of limitation that oppose the accomplishment of His will. While we have a role to play in responding to God's word, we must realize that we are never alone in our struggles; God is always with us. (See, for example, Matthew 28:20.) He requires our effort, but He provides His grace to help us overcome our weaknesses and uncertainties.

In the next few chapters, we will explore the various obstacles we face while attempting to respond to God's voice, and we will discover some biblical solutions for removing them. Let us remember that whenever we feel frail, and our limitations seem insurmountable, we have a heavenly Father who assures us, *"My grace is sufficient for you, for my power is made perfect in weakness"* (2 Corinthians 12:9).

15

BREAKING THE GRIP
OF SELF-CONSCIOUSNESS

In the blockbuster movie *Superman*, the film's namesake and protagonist was undaunted by any challenge or opponent that stood in the way of his unwavering commitment to use his superhuman ability for the benefit of anyone in need. But while his otherworldly ability made him unstoppable and allowed him to do what others only dreamed of doing, there was one weapon used by his enemies that rendered him powerless—the substance "kryptonite," which reduced the commanding hero to a feeble mortal.

Similarly, as we seek to live according to God's plans for us, pursuing our miraculous potential, we face many strength-robbing challenges, but very few are as potent as self-consciousness. For many of us, a preoccupation with ourselves is what kryptonite is to Superman, having the ability to cripple the work of God through us. I have seen this formidable challenge render the most gifted, intelligent, and able individuals useless once they are in its fierce grasp. Despite clear direction from God, encouragement from other people, and open doors of opportunity, they cannot seem to get past their personal insecurities, pessimistic views of themselves, and worries about how they will appear to others if they respond to God's divine inspiration.

The God-given business concepts that are still only ideas, the books that have not yet been written, and the movements of God that remain only internal inspirations rather than external manifestations are casualties of this potential-deterring element. Unplanted churches, unsaved friends, unhealed communities, and uninspired humanity can also be linked to our inability to get beyond our own self-consciousness.

Why are we human beings so self-conscious? While there are certainly psychological, sociological, and emotional elements that are contributing factors, the origins of this common first response to God's speaking can be traced back to the events following the creation of humanity. It is worth noting that whenever we read the first few chapters of the book of Genesis, we are not simply reading a story about God's creative genius but peering into His original intent for humankind. Here we can find foundational insights for marriage, for the family, and for humanity's purpose. We can also note historical, philosophical, anthropological, and spiritual implications.

Additionally, in these chapters we are able to examine the effects of mankind's original failure and the residue from it, which remains with us to this day. Let's briefly review what transpired. God instructed Adam that he could eat of any tree in the garden of Eden except *"the tree of the knowledge of good and evil."* (See Genesis 2:16–17.) But it wasn't long before both Adam and his wife, Eve, disobeyed that instruction. This first act of disobedience to God—which has come to be called "the fall of humanity"—and the results that followed are recorded in Genesis 3:6–7:

> *When the woman saw that the fruit of the tree was good for food and pleasing to the eye, and also desirable for gaining wisdom, she took some and ate it. She also gave some to her husband, who was with her, and he ate it. Then the eyes of both of them were opened, and they realized they were naked;*

so they sewed fig leaves together and made coverings for
themselves.

A NEW KIND OF AWARENESS

Interestingly, when some teachers explain the above passage,
they cite Adam and Eve's desire to cover themselves up as the first
act following their disobedience. However, before they sewed the
fig leaves together, covered themselves, and hid from God (see verse
8), they first experienced a heightened self-consciousness—*"they*
realized they were naked" (Genesis 3:7). We often focus on their
realization of their physical nakedness (the outward manifestation)
and overlook their awakened self-consciousness (the more important, internal process and its results). They became soberly aware of
themselves (self-conscious), and this awareness eclipsed the voice
and purposes of God in their lives. Their new perception led to all
of their subsequent actions.

Prior to this event, Adam and Eve heard God's voice, carried
out His instructions, and enjoyed His presence and one another's
company. This pattern was and still is the desire of God for His
people. We have already established that it is God's will to speak to
His children and for them to respond to Him. We have also firmly
established the foundational importance of the law of Christ—
loving God and loving our neighbors as ourselves. Before the fall,
these realities were completely intact; Adam and Eve lived by God's
instructions while loving Him and one another. Their disobedience
robbed them of their ability to experience these things in an uninterrupted manner. Instead, they became preoccupied with their
own self-images, eclipsing the pattern previously established.

Thus, the fall wedged self (-consciousness) in between God's
instruction and their obedience. They now had to attempt to follow
God's words with a full view of their fallen selves and were reduced

to living with this ever-present issue of debilitating self-consciousness. The dynamics of human interaction changed, as well. The first human beings not only worried about their image before God but also about their image before one another. While they were still called to fulfill their godly assignments, they performed them with feelings of apprehension over how they appeared in the eyes of others.

A SENSE OF INADEQUACY

Though this dynamic was first experienced by Adam and Eve, its unmistakable residue has persevered through the ages. One of the greatest impediments to our obedient response to the words God speaks to us is our preoccupation with our image in relation to Him, to ourselves, and to others. The story of the prophet Jeremiah gives us a clear example of this:

> Now the word of the LORD came to me [Jeremiah] saying, "Before I formed you in the womb I knew you, and before you were born I consecrated you; I have appointed you a prophet to the nations." Then I said, "Alas, Lord GOD! Behold, I do not know how to speak, because I am a youth." But the LORD said to me, "Do not say, 'I am a youth,' because everywhere I send you, you shall go, and all that I command you, you shall speak. Do not be afraid of them, for I am with you to deliver you," declares the LORD.   (Jeremiah 1:4–8 NASB)

In the passage above, the word of the Lord comes compellingly to Jeremiah and clearly reveals the will of the God of heaven for his life. The Lord cites three things in this short scriptural selection: (1) He was intimately acquainted with Jeremiah before his birth. (2) Jeremiah had a purpose for which he was consecrated. (3) Jeremiah was called to be a prophet to the nations. Interestingly, this announcement produced pushback in Jeremiah rather than agreement. His response to

God's divine utterance was, *"Alas, Lord GOD! Behold, I do not know how to speak, because I am a youth"* (Jeremiah 1:6 NASB). At that moment, there was a standoff between the divine and the ordinary, the infinite and the finite, the Creator and the created.

Here we see a unique problem that persists to this day, and with just as much crippling potency. The same standoff can be observed in God's dealings with others throughout Scripture, and it is present in the lives of believers today who struggle with obediently responding to God's voice. I call this purpose-hindering stalemate "the battle of declarations." Whenever God speaks a word of direction and we refuse to act on it or agree with it, we officially move into this deadlock. While our lives and activities may continue, our miraculous possibilities are thwarted.

There is something about God's marvelousness and the exalted nature of His speaking that causes us to see the pronounced finiteness of our own nature. As a result of their self-consciousness, one of the most frequent responses of people who receive instruction from the Lord, who encounter His glory, or who hear His voice is to look at their own inadequacies. We see our own frailties and miss His sufficiency and desire to work through us. This is an innate flaw in our operating system that leads us to doubt before we believe, to focus on our own limited ability as opposed to our strength in Him, and to become fixated on our challenges and not our opportunities.

While this is a common human experience, such a response is never God's ultimate goal for us. Our sense of the wonder of God is to be held in tandem with a sense of the *possibilities* for us and others when we come into agreement with His purposes. His speaking is never meant to leave us discouraged by the thought of how wretched we are in comparison to His vision for our lives but rather how amazing we can be when empowered by Him.

Because God's desire is to co-labor with mankind to accomplish His purposes on earth, there is a place not only for divine initiation but also for human participation. If both of these elements are not fully functional, miraculous outcomes will be frustrated. Human activity that is not inspired by God is limited in power and authority. On the other hand, divine revelation without human agreement lacks the embodiment that allows much of the will of God to manifest itself in the physical world. This is why one of Satan's most potent attacks is on human agreement with divine plans. He cannot stop God's end of the equation, so he targets the believer with a sense of inadequacy, doubts, fears, and reminders of past sins and failures. He employs these methods in an attempt to get us to disqualify what God has qualified.

Even without any external discouragement, our internal, personal view of ourselves can be the greatest impediment to our obedient surrender to God's will. Our heightened awareness of self, amid God's direction and guidance, regularly robs us of our motivation and can eclipse the eternal purposes of God for our lives.

THE TRUTHS THAT GOD KNOWS ABOUT US

Without question, our best reaction would be to simply agree with or respond positively to God whenever we receive a word from Him concerning who we are or what we are to do. Our motivation for this response should not be fear of being punished by Him if we disobey, or of missing out on His blessings, but rather that He knows the truth about us and our circumstances, and He has the superior declaration. The words of the Lord that preceded Jeremiah's protest hold the key to the wisdom of a yielded, rather than resistive, posture.

HE KNEW US BEFORE WE WERE BORN

The first reason for us to yield when we are in a standoff with God is found in Jeremiah 1:5 (NASB), where God declares, *"Before I formed you in the womb I knew you...."* This statement suggests that it would be wise to come into agreement with God's declarations because of His intimate acquaintance with who we are, which was a reality before we ever existed. In other words, though we are daily becoming more familiar with who we truly are in Christ, God fully knew who we are and what we would become before any of us were even formed in our mothers' wombs.

If God calls us strong, intelligent, blessed, mighty, righteous, powerful, supplied, and so on, we must agree. The reason for our surrender to His declaration is that it is never spoken from a place of superficial optimism, of casual acquaintance with us, or of obscured vision of who we really are. Instead, it is generated from the vision He had of us from the beginning. He is, without doubt, more familiar with our tomorrows than we are with our yesterdays. This is why the Lord immediately corrects Jeremiah's feeble response with an ascended and prophetic one. As Jeremiah cowers, saying, *"I do not know how to speak, because I am a youth"* (Jeremiah 1:6 NASB), God responds, *"Do not say, 'I am a youth,' because everywhere I send you, you shall go, and all that I command you, you shall speak"* (verse 7 NASB). The Lord was saying, in essence, "Do not say about yourself what I do not say about you." His words imply, "You are who I say you are." They also indicate, "You can do what I say you can."

HIS ENABLEMENT ALWAYS FOLLOWS HIS DIRECTIVES

While the declaration *"I am [only] a youth"* (Jeremiah 1:6 NASB) was linked to Jeremiah's identity issues, the protestation *"I do not know how to speak"* (verse 7 NASB) was related to his perception of his abilities. Most of our greatest doubts surrounding our miraculous potential are rooted in challenges related to our identity or ability. The fact that Jeremiah's identity was established by God before he was born takes away his right to disqualify himself based on his own feelings. Similarly, God's reply, *"Everywhere*

I send you, you shall go, and all that I command you, you shall speak"
(Jeremiah 1:7 NASB), counters Jeremiah's apprehensions about his
ability. This portion of the passage reminds us that God's divine
enablement always follows His utterances of direction. So when
God's word calls us beyond the barriers of our self-constructed
limitations, "I agree" or "Amen" is always the fitting response.

CHRIST'S SACRIFICE COVERS OUR SINS AND FAILURES

Sadly, many people live beneath their possibilities in God each
day because of their inability to come into agreement with Him
when He speaks. Again, this is not a new challenge for human
beings but one that can be traced in God's encounters with people
throughout Scripture. Moses responded to God's word with insecurity and doubt when the Lord called him to deliver His people
from slavery in Egypt. (See Exodus 3:1–11.) Gideon questioned
his pedigree and low place in his family when God declared him
to be a *"mighty warrior"* and the deliverer of Israel from the hand
of the Midianites. (See Judges 6:11–15.) Jeremiah, though supernaturally encountered by God, chose at first to doubt the word of
the Lord due to his own overshadowing, defeatist view of himself and his shortcomings. It was then—and still is—humanity's
self-consciousness that roadblocks our progress toward our miraculous potential. We often see the direction God desires for us
to move in but find that our vision of that reality becomes eclipsed
by our skewed perception of ourselves.

Due to our previous mistakes or failures in life (a topic we will
explore further in a later chapter), we often struggle with feeling
inadequate to carry out God's will, even though we know Christ's
sacrifice covers our every sin. This is because knowing it in theory
and wholeheartedly living in its reality are two separate things.
This awareness of our past weaknesses and the future possibility of
failure can cause us to abdicate or even reject our response to God's

word. This is why the writings of the New Testament focus on the idea of Christ's substitution on our behalf, on believers as "new creations" in Jesus, and on the foundational principle of "death to self." "Self," in this sense, represents a life or a will that is living independently of God's will and instructions.

The fall of humanity caused the eyes of Adam and his wife to be taken off of God and placed on themselves. But again, the sacrifice of Christ deals with the issue of our guilt and shame once and for all so that we may take our eyes off of our condition and fix them back on God. In Christ, we can now follow His pattern by fixing our gaze on the Father. This is why Christ declared in John 5:19 (NASB), *"Truly, truly, I say to you, the Son can do nothing of Himself, unless it is something He sees the Father doing; for whatever the Father does, these things the Son also does in like manner."* Here Jesus doesn't speak about the process of being led by God as "hearing" but as "seeing." I believe this implies that He lived a life that was reversing the effects of the fall. In His perfect humanity, He was modeling for us a key to the miraculous existence, which, again, is to lift our eyes off of ourselves—radically abandoning self-consciousness by allowing it to be drowned in God-consciousness. While our journey or path is not marked by perfection, as Jesus' was, we can still fix our eyes on God and not ourselves because His sacrifice completely removed our sin from us, rendering our present guilt for past (repented of) offenses impotent. Therefore, whenever God instructs us, we must fix our eyes on Him—and not on ourselves—and respond.

OUR STANDING IS SECURE BEFORE GOD AND OTHER PEOPLE

As with Adam and Eve, our self-consciousness not only interferes with our ability to respond to God, based on a sense of inadequacy, but it also challenges our capacity to function naturally before other people in obedience to His word. Adam and Eve covered themselves up *before* hearing God approach them in the garden after their disobedience. At that moment, there was no one physically present except the two of them. Self-consciousness was therefore present in their human relationship before God entered the scene. This self-consciousness came with the burden of anxiety over how they were viewed by one another. Like Adam and Eve, many of us today constantly think about how we are perceived in the eyes of others. As a result, when God speaks a word of direction to us, it first has to pass through a litany of the real or hypothetical opinions of others.

While it is always wise to consider the effects of our actions on other people, refusing to respond to a God-given word due to our self-consciousness before others limits our miraculous potential. For many people, a concern over how they are perceived by family members, friends, coworkers, and others is more difficult to overcome than the challenge of their self-consciousness before God. It is often easier for us to cave in to the disapproval of people whom we can see than to obey a God whom we can't see. One reason is that while other people's indictments usually come to us directly and clearly, God's indictments generally have to be discerned.

People's judgmental tone of voice, opinions, and rejection can, without question, produce a powerful and lingering effect on us. This is why Jeremiah had to be reminded by the Lord, after receiving His word and assignment, *"Do not be afraid of them, for I am with you to deliver you"* (Jeremiah 1:8). In fact, the first chapter of Jeremiah concludes with further words from God designed to build the prophet's confidence in responding to the original word of the Lord:

> *Now behold, I have made you today as a fortified city and as a pillar of iron and as walls of bronze against the whole land, to the kings of Judah, to its princes, to its priests and to the people of the land. They will fight against you, but they will not overcome you, for I am with you to deliver you.*
>
> (Jeremiah 1:18–19 NASB)

I cannot begin to express how often the plans of the Lord through His people remain unrealized because of their heightened concern for what other people may think of them. Questions like "How will I be viewed?" "What will it do to my reputation?" and "What will people think if I fail?" are pondered by most reasoning people. Self-consciousness causes us to become fixated on these and other destiny-hindering questions. While such thoughts are natural considerations and are to be expected, they should never keep us from responding to the word of the Lord. Excessive attentiveness to self and overly questioning one's standing when attempting to respond to a word or idea from God is paralyzing.

SELFLESS OBEDIENCE

Interestingly, it is *selfless* obedience to God that builds in us a confidence and security in our spiritual journeys and lays the groundwork for miraculous results. Can you imagine how liberating it would be to respond to God's voice without the self-consciousness associated with our past mistakes or failures? This is what the first human beings experienced in the garden of Eden before the fall. And again, it is what the Lord still desires for His children today. Of course, receiving the Lord's word should produce in us a sacred sobriety; however, we shouldn't allow our awe and reverence toward Him to produce an unhealthy self-consciousness before Him. The knowledge of Christ's sacrifice for us and our new identity in Him should generate in us a boldness to respond to the will of God based on *Jesus'* standing with God—and ours in Him—and not on our own track record of past deeds or misdeeds.

From the very beginning, the original intent of the Lord was to speak words of life and instruction to His children that would be obediently carried out by them—without a preoccupation with self-image depriving them of their confidence before Him or others. When we return to this original posture—unbound by self-consciousness—it takes us out of the center of the equation and makes the presence and instruction of the Lord central. This is why the apostle Paul considered himself a "dead man" to his old life, so that he now lived for the purposes, instruction, and direction of Christ. He wrote, *"I have been crucified with Christ and I no longer live, but Christ lives in me"* (Galatians 2:20). When Paul's personal will or view of himself conflicted with God's instruction or definition of who he was, he did not give himself too much latitude to debate over it or to allow the opinions of others to deter him from listening to God. Instead, he counted himself as a *"crucified"* man who embodied and obediently responded to the word of the Lord. Although, like anyone else, he felt the full spectrum of human emotion, he did not allow self (-consciousness) to sabotage his response to the will of God. Because of this, he did not live beneath his possibilities but realized his full miraculous potential.

OVERCOMING SELF-CONSCIOUSNESS

The above insights are easier to grasp cognitively than they are to act upon. Here are some practical steps that can aid us in the process of learning to overcome our self-consciousness.

SAY WHAT GOD SAYS ABOUT YOU

The first step to overcoming the self-consciousness that too often restricts our obedient response to God is to understand and repeat what He says concerning us. While Jeremiah had the seeming advantage of personally receiving a dramatic declaration from the Lord, we can receive God's perspective of us by reading and studying the whole of His written Word. When thoughts of our inadequacies and supposed shaky standing before Him creep into our minds, we can refute them with dominant, positive declarations found in Scripture. Despite our feelings, God's truthful declarations must always take precedence over our feeble declarations.

One of the best ways to build ourselves up in the truth is to not only read the Word but also voice it aloud, so that we can hear it. This method will condition our minds to view reality from God's perspective and not our own. It will also allow His proclamations to dominate our self-talk. Romans 12:2 (NLT) declares, *"Don't copy the behavior and customs of this world, but let God transform you into a new person by changing the way you think ["by the renewing of your mind" NIV]."* Second Corinthians 10:5 takes things even further by revealing that a renewed mind (thinking like God) requires effort on our part, stating, *"We take captive every thought to make it obedient to Christ."* In other words, our thoughts and perspectives do not match God's just because we are His children but must be brought into obedient compliance with them. We must therefore say and believe what God says about us.

ARTICULATE GOD'S PERSPECTIVE TO OTHERS

Another strategy that is helpful for acting in the face of self-consciousness is to articulate to others the word God has spoken to you. This practice moves God's instruction and your mental deliberation over it out of your head and into a more public realm. Accordingly, God paints a picture in the book of Habakkuk of how His revelation is to be stewarded. He does not allow the prophet to simply treasure the word in his heart, or to deliberate over it internally, but instructs him, *"Write down the revelation and make it plain on tablets so that a herald may run with it"* (Habakkuk 2:2).

Even though God's word to Habakkuk was declared in a specific context, its truth still has a tremendous amount of application for us. First, as we discussed in earlier chapters, taking an internal revelation and putting it on paper somehow helps to crystallize God's word in our lives. This process *"make[s] it plain"* and undercuts our ability to alter, negotiate with, or compromise an obedient response to God's instruction. Moreover, entrusting the contents of the divine message to "heralds" (those who proclaim a message on behalf of another) makes it much more difficult for us to shrink back from what God has instructed us to do. Although we may still struggle with a degree of self-consciousness, the act of revealing a spiritual mandate publically somehow aids in breaking the intimidation factor that stifles our response to God's word.

We must be mindful of what environments we introduce a word of the Lord into in the early stages of its unfolding. However, sharing it with those in your circle of trust can be invaluable. When you articulate His word to others, you now have people in your life who can remind you of your strength in God to perform the task, despite your own insecurities. Sharing the word also gives you the opportunity to be accountable to others who can check your progress in the event they see little or no movement toward the fulfillment of that word. Additionally, letting your true friends know what God has spoken to you grants them the opportunity to encourage you and pray for you, especially if you have to function in a setting where many of the people around you may not be as gracious toward God's words or works.

Though we may pride ourselves on our independence and spiritual fortitude, the reality is that we need the support of a small group of like-minded people when attempting to carry out God's will in the culture at large. The members of this small community can continually remind us of God's perspective and celebrate with us the victories that society may frown upon or resist. Although miraculous events can take place through the life of an individual who functions independently of others, a miraculous life is sustained in spiritual community.

JUMP IN WITH BOTH FEET

At the end of the day, we may never have 100 percent confidence or 0 percent self-consciousness. However, heaven and earth are waiting for our miraculous potential to be released through our obedient response to the Lord's utterances. That being said, there comes a time when we must jump in with both feet, despite how we feel!

I have a close relative who is known to sit poolside without ever getting into the water. While she is usually adorned with designer swimsuits, colorful swimming caps, professional nose plugs, and Olympic-quality goggles, she rarely, if ever, participates in any aquatic activities. Beyond her general concern about damaging her salon-styled hair, there is a fundamental flaw in her approach. While I believe she truly desires to swim with the rest of us, she refuses to ever just jump into the water. Instead, she gauges its temperature by dipping one toe in, and then immediately shivering and jumping backward with the high-pitched words, "It's too cold!" All of us who have already braved the initial shock of the cold water shout to her, "It's not bad once you jump in; your body will get used to it!" In response, she briefly protests and then goes back to sitting on a deck chair, fully clothed with swimming attire.

My relative's approach to swimming serves as a parallel to the timidity that often characterizes our response to God's speaking. Like attempting to gradually slide into a cold pool one body part at a time, trying to gradually respond to a challenging word from God can also prove futile. Our delayed or gradual response allows time for more doubts, fears, and questions to splash over us. These times of testing the waters rarely lead to a faith-filled experience, but they do often lead to cowering backward into complacency. We end up merely sitting beside the miraculous while observing others enjoying the benefits of radical obedience, immersed in His purposes and blessings.

Those who leap with both feet into the will of God find that it is rarely as challenging as they thought it would be, and they are grateful they did. In contrast, those who constantly remain on the sidelines usually look back over their lives and wish they had been bold enough to jump in, because deep down they know they are not living up to their divine potential. Even more heartrending is the idea that, like my fully-bedecked family member, we would stay on the sidelines while divinely clothed with the spiritual gifts, wisdom, and strength necessary for any task the Lord instructs us to perform.

16

SUCCEEDING AS A DIVINE MANAGER

By recognizing the negative effects that self-consciousness and past failures and disappointments inflict on us as we seek to obey a word from God, we can free ourselves from these hindrances and begin to walk in our miraculous potential. Yet there are additional factors that can stall our response to God's revealed purposes for us, which we will explore in the next two chapters. The first topic is our sense of stewardship over what God has entrusted to us.

Whether it is a resource we are meant to put into use, a ministry for which we are responsible to provide oversight, or even a specific revelation, we are held accountable for the way we respond. I believe this is particularly true of the words God speaks to us. The following passage, known as "the parable of the talents," serves as an excellent illustration of how to respond when entrusted by God—"*the master*"—with anything. Jesus said,

> For [God's kingdom] *is just like a man about to go on a journey, who called his own slaves and entrusted his possessions to them. To one he gave five talents, to another, two, and to another, one, each according to his own ability; and he went on his journey. Immediately the one who had received the five talents went and traded with them, and gained five more talents.*

In the same manner the one who had received the two talents gained two more. But he who received the one talent went away, and dug a hole in the ground and hid his master's money. Now after a long time the master of those slaves came and settled accounts with them. The one who had received the five talents came up and brought five more talents, saying, "Master, you entrusted five talents to me. See, I have gained five more talents." His master said to him, "Well done, good and faithful slave. You were faithful with a few things, I will put you in charge of many things; enter into the joy of your master." Also the one who had received the two talents came up and said, "Master, you entrusted two talents to me. See, I have gained two more talents." His master said to him, "Well done, good and faithful slave. You were faithful with a few things, I will put you in charge of many things; enter into the joy of your master." And the one also who had received the one talent came up and said, "Master, I knew you to be a hard man, reaping where you did not sow and gathering where you scattered no seed. And I was afraid, and went away and hid your talent in the ground. See, you have what is yours." But his master answered and said to him, "You wicked, lazy slave, you knew that I reap where I did not sow and gather where I scattered no seed. Then you ought to have put my money in the bank, and on my arrival I would have received my money back with interest. Therefore take away the talent from him, and give it to the one who has the ten talents. For to everyone who has, more shall be given, and he will have an abundance; but from the one who does not have, even what he does have shall be taken away. Throw out the worthless slave into the outer darkness; in that place there will be weeping and gnashing of teeth."   (Matthew 25:14–30 NASB)

As we noted in an earlier chapter, Jesus concluded His discussion of a different parable—the parable of the sower—with the same tagline that we find in the above parable: *"For whoever has, to him more shall be given, and he will have an abundance; but whoever does not have, even what he has shall be taken away from him"* (Matthew 13:12 NASB). I believe the two passages in Matthew are meant to be parallel in every way, the only exception being what was specifically left in the servants' care in each parable. In Matthew 25, the talents, or measure of money, given by the master to his servants, are symbolically representative of everything God entrusts to our care. The resource given in the earlier passage from Matthew 13 was not talents but rather *"the word of the kingdom"* (Matthew 13:19 NASB), entrusted to all those who hear it. While the scope in Matthew 13 is narrowed to the revelation given by God, I believe it is meant to carry the sense of Matthew 25 in every way. Thus, every principle from Jesus' parable of the talents can be applied to His parable of the sower. (We will explore the parable of the sower in more detail in the next chapter of this book.) The keen insights in the parable of the talents therefore give us greater perspective on how to treat Jesus' words and how to respond to them. They also reveal certain things that keep us from properly responding.

THE PRINCIPLE OF STEWARDSHIP

The parable first establishes the principle of stewardship: *"Just like a man about to go on a journey, who called his own slaves and **entrusted** his possessions to them"* (Matthew 25:14 NASB). A steward is a person employed to handle the resources of another. Every person who properly handles God's words carries the sense that they do not own them but instead are called to be the administrator of them. This mind-set creates a sense of responsibility for how they handle what has been assigned to their care. Stewards realize that they have a certain degree of autonomy to oversee the resource they've been given, but they also know they will have to give an account for how they have administered it. So one of the motivating factors of our faithful response to God's instruction should be that we are held accountable not for what we've heard and received but what we have done with what we've heard and received.

DIFFERENCES IN MANAGING RESOURCES

The parable goes on to cite the differences between those who responded properly to their stewardship and the one who responded foolishly. The significant difference is that those who were good stewards made it their business to be intentional about what they did with what they had received. On the other hand, although the foolish manager didn't lose what he was given, he simply did nothing with it. How many of us marvel over words or direction we've been given by God but never move beyond the revelation stage to the implementation stage? The indictment against us is that, like the foolish servant, we don't even try.

How many words of direction or instruction from God are buried in the recesses of our hearts? Again, they may be business plans, ideas for books, concepts for ministry initiatives, or other God-breathed ideas—but they are all buried! We often celebrate the fact that God has spoken to us, but celebrating a spoken word without moving forward to implement it is like throwing your hands up in victory on the third lap of a one-mile race when you still have one lap to go. The reason the word was spoken in the first place was so that you would respond to what was being entrusted to your care. While the initial words that God speaks are significant, remember that, in the parable of the sower, God's word is depicted as "*seeds.*" In order for the greater harvest to be realized, there must be a correct response by the recipients of those seeds. The parable reveals that our active response is essential.

FAULTY THINKING LEADS TO POOR MANAGEMENT

The parable of the talents not only creates a contrast between the faithful stewards and the foolish steward, but it also gives us insight into the internal thought processes of the one who misman-aged the master's resource (or words). A brief review of the follow-ing verses will reveal a few of the hindrances that can keep us from responding positively when God speaks to us.

> *And the one also who had received the one talent came up and said, "Master, I knew you to be a hard man, reaping where you did not sow and gathering where you scattered no seed. And I was afraid, and went away and hid your talent in the ground. See, you have what is yours." But his master answered and said to him, "You wicked, lazy slave, you knew that I reap where I did not sow and gather where I scattered no seed...."*
> (Matthew 25:24–26 NASB)

We find much of this unfaithful steward's problem revealed in his own words, and we discover the rest of the problem in the language of the master.

A DEFEATED PERSPECTIVE

The first weakness that kept the servant from properly responding was a defeated perspective. He told the master the reason for his inac-tivity: *"I knew you to be a hard man..."* (Matthew 25:24 NASB). What caused him to cower in the face of difficulty as opposed to flourish-ing in it? Why did he allow the fires of his situation to consume him instead of using them as motivational fuel to accelerate his pace? In the above passage, two out of the three people responded properly. The other two may have seen the master's shrewdness as a challenge but used it as incentive to perform rather than to wilt. The mere fact that two others did something with what they were given takes away the excuse of the one who did nothing.

If what God requires of me has ever been done by anyone else who has walked the face of the earth, then it's in the realm of possi-bility. It is still possible even if it *hasn't* been done before, because God has commanded it, but we should take courage from the examples of others. Oftentimes, they are the proof that it can be done.

One of the methods I use to motivate myself when challenged by God to do what I feel is beyond me is to ask myself, "Has this been done before by anyone else?" If the answer is yes, somehow the task doesn't seem as daunting. And, if two out of three people have accomplished it (a majority), that's even more encouraging. Many of us are fearful of doing what we have so many examples of others around us accomplishing. There are people less intelligent, gifted, and knowledgeable than we are who have accomplished twice as much as we have. If we are going to experience all God has for us, we must be bold in our response to His speaking, taking courage from the boldness and successes of others. Learn to see challenges as motivation for action as opposed to an opportunity to make excuses.

A FEARFUL OUTLOOK

While it's easy to talk about the need to be bold, it can be difficult to actually respond with boldness. The major reason for this is revealed in the next statement given by the steward: *"I was afraid"* (Matthew 25:25). The reality is that fear robs us of an immediate—or even an eventual—response to a word God has given us. How many times have we conveniently shelved a God-idea, a divine inspiration, or a word from the Lord simply because we were afraid? Afraid that things wouldn't work out as we hoped. Afraid we would be embarrassed by failure. Fearful God wouldn't do His part. I've even met individuals who were terror-stricken by the thought of what they would do if they succeeded. It's important to understand that feelings of trepidation are often a normal part of responding to a new and challenging word from God. Generally, people who respond boldly aren't those who don't feel the same fear as others—they've just learned how to function despite their fear.

LAZINESS

There is one last barrier to a proper response to stewardship, this time articulated by the master. After listening to the unfaithful steward's excuses, he called him *"lazy"* (Matthew 25:26). While I wish I could find a kinder way to express this indictment, I just can't. The reality is that many of us have to be honest with ourselves and others and admit that we struggle with this frailty. The group Alcoholics Anonymous states that the first step to recovery is admitting we have a problem. Conversely, the easiest way to ensure that we will stay in bondage is denial. I find very few people who will admit they are just flat-out lazy. It is easier to blame our circumstances on our boss, coworker, upbringing, circumstances, lack of resources, or even God. While some of these things may play a role, we have to learn to identify and address the areas in our lives that need adjusting, including laziness. Many of us need to confront our laziness head-on. For example, while some people have physical conditions that make it more difficult for them to function than others, laziness in this context is not so much physiological as it is psychological.

Many factors contribute to what we would identify as laziness; however, I will highlight just a few.

WE DON'T WANT TO BE 'INCONVENIENCED'

First, I believe many people find themselves moving into laziness and inactivity because they are unwilling to experience the inconvenience associated with their God-given task or assignment. It is easier (for spiritual people in particular, it seems) to treasure something in theory or in its abstract form rather than to actually work when necessary to produce the desired outcome. Dr. Neel Burton, in his article "The Psychology of Laziness," writes that a person is lazy "if his motivation to spare himself effort trumps his motivation to do the right or expected thing."[6] Our addiction to comfort and convenience, and our inability to delay gratification, can cause us to become complacent when we should be producing. For the foolish steward, somehow the long-term settling of accounts with the master or the reality of what the future would be like for him if he didn't produce wasn't enough to prompt him to action on a daily basis. Similarly, when we become lazy, it is because we have lost sight of the ultimate consequences of our inactivity.

WE DON'T FEEL OUR EFFORTS ARE 'REWARDING' ENOUGH

Second, we can become lazy when the practical, daily tasks necessary to respond to God's instruction don't feel rewarding. Notice that the other stewards' rewards for their wise decisions didn't come daily but *"after a long time"* (Matthew 25:19) when the master returned. Our response to God's word doesn't always give immediate rewards or supply frequent goose bumps of excitement; sometimes it can feel very routine and practical. When their efforts no longer seem rewarding or stimulating, many people opt out by shifting to something that is less rigorous but immediately gratifying. If this describes you, I encourage you to admit to a degree of laziness and put your hands back to the work God has called you to; reward, gratification, fulfillment, and results will eventually come to those who faithfully respond to Him daily.

WE HOLD ON TO PERFECTIONISM

Third, laziness and inactivity can be attributed to a seemingly unlikely source, and that is perfectionism. I have found that it is not only fearful or comfort-seeking people who can be ineffective but also some of the most committed, gifted people on the face of

---

6, See https://www.psychologytoday.com/blog/hide-and-seek/201410/the-psychology-laziness.

the planet. The reason for their inactivity is their perfectionism or need to control the outcomes.

Ecclesiastes 11:4 (NASB) states, *"He who watches the wind will not sow and he who looks at the clouds will not reap."* This is a picture of a farmer standing at the threshold of his door with seed in his hand but never leaving the house because the wind looks too severe. Then, when he finally does get the seed in the ground and the harvest is produced, he stands at the same threshold and refuses to reap his harvest because there is the possibility of rain. This passage is simply stating that those who wait for the perfect circumstances before acting rarely act. In this life, perfect circumstances rarely come, but our response to God cannot be delayed due to imperfect conditions. Heaven and earth await the miraculous harvest produced by our simple acts of obedience.

17

REAPING A MIRACULOUS HARVEST

The parable of the sower, like the parable of the talents, gives us insights into how we should hear and respond to divine utterances from God. While the context of the parable is the message of God's kingdom, the illustrations reveal obstacles we encounter whenever we attempt to respond to any word God speaks to us.

Let us begin by reviewing this parable:

Behold, the sower went out to sow; and as he sowed, some seeds fell beside the road, and the birds came and ate them up. Others fell on the rocky places, where they did not have much soil; and immediately they sprang up, because they had no depth of soil. But when the sun had risen, they were scorched; and because they had no root, they withered away. Others fell among the thorns, and the thorns came up and choked them out. And others fell on the good soil and yielded a crop, some a hundredfold, some sixty, and some thirty. He who has ears, let him hear. (Matthew 13:3–9 NASB)

The following is Jesus' interpretation of the parable:

When anyone hears the word of the kingdom and does not understand it, the evil one comes and snatches away what has been sown in his heart. This is the one on whom seed was sown beside the road. The one on whom seed was sown on the rocky places, this is the man who hears the word and immediately receives it with joy; yet he has no firm root in himself, but is only temporary, and when affliction or persecution arises because of the word, immediately he falls away. And the one on whom seed was sown among the thorns, this is the man who hears the word, and the worry of the world and the deceitfulness of wealth choke the word, and it becomes unfruitful. And the one on whom seed was sown on the good soil, this is the man who hears the word and understands it; who indeed bears fruit and brings forth, some a hundredfold, some sixty, and some thirty. (Matthew 13:19–23 NASB)

Again, the seeds scattered by the farmer represent the message of God's kingdom or His words. The types of soil represent the internal makeup of the various individuals who hear His message. The first three kinds of "soil," which are not conducive to long-term growth, are contrasted with the *"good soil,"* which produces substantial results based on God's message being heard, understood, and acted upon. The parable implies that in order to be *"good soil"* (an individual who properly responds to God's word and experiences its benefits), we must not allow the issues that hindered the first three types of "soil" to hinder us. It lets us know that some major potential roadblocks to a healthy response to God's message are a lack of understanding, a superficial acceptance of His word, and an allowance of smothering influences in our lives, such as the distraction of worry and the deceitfulness of riches.

ROADBLOCKS TO MIRACULOUS RESULTS

A LACK OF UNDERSTANDING

In the parable, the first roadblock to the miraculous is pictured as a seed that fell along the road and was snatched away by birds.

The Lord interprets the roadside as the individual who hears the word but has no understanding concerning it. It is understanding that causes the words of the Master to penetrate more deeply into our hearts. There is no doubt that the Lord will require some things of us in our lifetimes that are beyond our understanding; however, in general, the greater our understanding of God's word, the more deeply it is established in us, so that we experience greater productivity and can better implement His will.

While God does work in mysterious ways, it is shocking to me to see the passive behavior of many of His people in regard to those ways. The mystery of the Lord, or our lack of comprehension concerning His deeper purposes, was never meant to make us more passive in our journey of discovery toward the miraculous but instead more intrigued and explorative. As we saw earlier, Moses didn't understand everything about God, but he didn't use that as an excuse to become passive in his relationship with God or to accept his circumstances as his "human lot." Instead, he used it to ignite a prayer that expressed his desire: *"If you are pleased with me, teach me your ways so I may know you and continue to find favor with you"* (Exodus 33:13). We find King David with the same burning passion to delve deeper into an understanding of God. David declared, *"Make me know Your ways, O Lord; teach me Your paths. Lead me in Your truth and teach me"* (Psalm 25:4–5 NASB). Likewise, it was the seed of God's word, combined with a heart for discovery, that caused the early disciples of Jesus to leave their businesses and all they counted dear to learn from and come to know this Messiah who so captivated them.

This makes me ask, "Among believers today, where is our desire to deepen our understanding of God's ways?" If there is any hope of our experiencing the miraculous life or harvest that God desires for us, we must hear His voice, seek to gain an understanding of His message (when possible), and respond to His instruction. *"The beginning of wisdom is this: Get wisdom. Though it cost all you have, get understanding"* (Proverbs 4:7).

While I can't deal with the subject of Satan (depicted as birds in the parable) exhaustively in this book, it is important for us to understand that we do have an adversary that works tirelessly to prevent the plans of God from being accomplished. He can't prevent it at the Source, which is God Himself, so he works to discourage our response to God's will, knowing that much of the Father's work on earth is accomplished through His people. We are much easier targets for the enemy, and when we don't respond to God's instruction, we allow an atmosphere void of spiritual influence to be formed in our lives. This is why the enemy attempts to steal the word before we respond and release the harvest God desires. His primary method of theft is his lies, which contradict God's truth. They encourage us to entertain temptations so that we are distracted and prevented from pondering and understanding the things of God.

When we gain understanding and set our will to not only receive revelation but also respond to it, it is virtually impossible for the enemy to impede our progress. We must continually focus on the ideas, thoughts, and plans of God in order to combat the adversary's lies. The primary way we can do this is by allowing a constant stream of God's words to flow into our minds and hearts. God's Word will strengthen us in times of temptation and trial. Remember, Scripture is the definitive Word of God that cannot be disputed by any other source, including Satan. Learn to read God's Word, to understand it, and to put it into practice.

Although it's essential to be fortified by Scripture, it is also important not to attempt to stand against the enemy's temptation on our own. One of the keys to overcoming temptation is to let other mature believers support us in the process. The popular term for seeking and allowing this support is "being accountable." It is giving others permission to hold us to a standard and to check with us at any point in the process to see how well we are doing. Often, when we try to fight temptation in isolation, our deepest struggles are never addressed—and they may go unnoticed by others until it's too late.

I have two tiers of accountability in my life as spiritual safeguards. The first is what I call "relational accountability," which consists of peers who organically respond to me and are often the first to notice subtle shifts in the tone or content of my conversation, a decrease in my confidence level in regard to personal victory, and other such nuances. The other tier is what I call "authoritative accountability." I have others in my life who I may have less frequent interaction with but who often have greater spiritual influence with me than my other relationships. Those who I have relational accountability with I consider my brothers and sisters, while those who provide authoritative accountability I consider fathers and mothers. One group provides routine "diagnostics," while the other provides intervention, when necessary, to help me alter my behavior. If we're serious about not only hearing but also doing the will of God, we have to make sure we give ourselves every advantage to overcome the enemy's lies and temptations.

A SUPERFICIAL ACCEPTANCE OF GOD'S WORD

A second obstacle to faithfully responding to God's message is accepting His words superficially; this situation is pictured in the parable of the sower by the rocky soil. It isn't a depiction of an individual who fails to understand what he has heard as much as it is a portrait of one who understands God's word but doesn't commit to it. Such a person has *"no depth of soil"* (Matthew 13:5 NASB) and therefore *"no root"* (Matthew 13:6 NASB). In the Bible, the imagery of roots speaks of constancy and commitment over a protracted period.

People attempt to interact with God for various reasons. Some sincerely desire to do His will completely, devoting their lives to that purpose. Others simply find His words to be healing, inspiring, or even mentally stimulating. The weakness of the latter group usually isn't revealed in times of ease and convenience but in times of adversity. These individuals are without roots, without commitment, so they abandon God's kingdom message or another word of revelation whenever they experience opposition or difficulty associated with it. Rootless individuals also abandon God's cause when they find something more appealing or titillating to them personally. Unless we have roots, we cannot hope to experience miraculous harvests with any consistency.

Therefore, if you desire spiritual stability, consistency, and fruitfulness, you must develop a spiritual root system that is deeper than a superficial infatuation with hearing God speak to you. You must have a true commitment to His words. You don't just wake up one morning transformed into someone who faithfully obeys every word from God. The way you develop this deep commitment is to make every word and instruction from the Lord a priority. The practical expression of that reality is to make a clear decision and plan to somehow implement or incorporate into your life every utterance of God. I realize this may sound overwhelming, but I've found that whatever doesn't get prioritized in my life eventually gets shelved. However, when I prioritize something, everything else in my life has to adjust to it. Making something a priority creates commitment, and commitment grows roots.

AN ALLOWANCE OF CHOKING INFLUENCES

Jesus rounds off His descriptions of the roadblocks that prevent a fruitful response to the Lord with the illustration of thorns that choke out the seeds, or effectiveness, of God's Word in the life of the hearer, explaining that the thorns represent *"the worry of the world and the deceitfulness of wealth"* (Matthew 13:22 NASB). The picture here is of the seed (the Word) and the *"thorns"* (worries/riches) both fighting to use the same *"soil"* (you) in order to flourish. For one to flourish, the other must suffer; both can't exist successfully in one environment. This is why, for example, when we are consumed with worry, it is not only difficult to clearly hear from God, but it is almost impossible to maintain the faith necessary to step out in obedience to His speaking.

THE WORRY OF THE WORLD

When consumed with worry, an individual rarely has the free "bandwidth" necessary to make significant or fruitful strides in God's kingdom. Worry is a high-maintenance partner, demanding your attention at all times. It often consumes both your conscious and subconscious thoughts. This makes it extremely difficult to look past your own issues and see God's larger plan for your family, your social circle, your church, your community, and the world.

It's important to realize that worry has no positive attributes or value but has many detriments. While worry can't "add a cubit to your stature" (see Matthew 6:27 NKJV, KJV), add one year to your life, change your circumstances, or strengthen your resolve, it can limit your clarity, isolate you from key relationships, ruin your health, and take your focus off the work God wants to do through you. In my late adolescent years, I heard a simple definition of worry that I have made my own: "Worry is stress placed on outcomes that may never come." There is actual research to back that assertion. Dr. Robert Leahy, author of *The Worry Cure*, quantifies it with his findings: "'Typically, 85 percent of the things people worry about have a neutral or positive outcome,' he says. And the remaining 15 percent? 'Of those, 78 percent of people say, "Well, things didn't work out, but I handled it pretty well."'"[7]

---

7. Sarah Mahoney, "What, Me Worry? Never Again," Life Reimagined, AARP, https://lifereimagined.aarp.org/stories/3571-What-Me-Worry-Never-Again.

THE DECEITFULNESS OF RICHES

Like worry, an inordinate desire for riches is a consuming fire. It isn't that money itself is inherently wrong; in fact, money is a neutral commodity. The parable of the sower doesn't demonize riches but rather indicts the mind-set of making them our main priority. The challenge is when the acquisition of "more" becomes the motivating factor of our actions; at this point, we have succumbed to the deceitfulness of riches.

The reality is that when we make a desire for riches our priority, we will never feel we have enough. If, at some point, we don't learn to find contentment, the chase for more and more riches will become endless. This is why Jesus dogmatically stated, *"You cannot serve God and wealth"* (Luke 16:13 NASB).

OVERCOMING WORRY AND THE DECEITFULNESS OF RICHES

While, as we have seen, worry can be a high-maintenance partner, the deceitfulness of wealth is a partner that is never satisfied and will make you its servant if you allow it to. However, both of these traps produce the same result: the strangulation of God's Word in your life and of your obedient response to it, severely limiting the harvest that is waiting for you as the fulfillment of your miraculous potential. Here are a few practical helps for escaping the smothering pressure of worry and the deceitfulness of wealth.

First, whenever I find myself becoming consumed with worry, I like to find something humorous to laugh at. I can't explain why this helps, but "laughter does the heart good, like medicine." (See Proverbs 17:22.)

I also practice looking outside of my own circumstance to find someone who is in a similar but direr situation than my own, and then seek to minister to his or her needs. If I was worried about my finances and had only one dollar, I would find someone who was even more worried because they only had ten cents to their name, and I would give them a portion of my dollar. I'm using this exaggerated example to point out that it's not the amount we have that's important but rather our ability to give. If we can be a true blessing to someone else, even in the midst of our own difficult circumstances, our worry can be replaced by a sense of our value to God and His purposes in the world.

Finally, if I am too consumed by worry to completely dismiss it, I put limitations on my fear or anxiety by setting a concise time period during which I can focus on it; in other words, I give myself permission to mull over my concerns for a short period of time by making an "appointment" to do so. Outside of that time frame, I let go of the fear or anxiety. This approach keeps me from continually obsessing over worry, and it serves as a first step that helps me to manage my thought life. If I can corral my worry by learning to contain it, it can eventually be eradicated. The apostle Paul wrote,

> *Don't worry about anything; instead, pray about everything. Tell God what you need, and thank him for all he has done. Then you will experience God's peace, which exceeds anything we can understand. His peace will guard your hearts and minds as you live in Christ Jesus.*   (Philippians 4:6–7 NLT)

Here now are some practical principles for overcoming the deceitfulness of wealth. First, like Paul, learn to be content in whatever circumstances you're in. (See Philippians 4:11–12.) Being content doesn't mean you don't desire to better yourself; it just means you don't allow yourself to be consumed by thoughts of what you lack. Second, practice delayed gratification. This will aid in your ability to overcome a constant thirst for more. Learning to say no to something that you do have the ability to acquire gives you an unusual advantage—it frees you from being possessed by your possessions. Third, as we discussed in one of the remedies for worry, practice generosity and release some of what you own to someone else. Anything we can freely release, we will never be a slave to.

Successfully overcoming the obstacles highlighted by Jesus in the parable of the sower will position us not only to accurately receive God's words but also to actively respond to them, setting into motion unimaginable, miraculous results.

18

OVERCOMING FAILURES AND DISAPPOINTMENTS

As I mentioned while discussing self-consciousness, without question, one of the greatest obstacles to future obedience to God is past disappointments or failures. We humans love to embellish our strengths while minimizing our frailties, but the reality is that we are much more sensitive about regret and failure in our lives than we are willing to admit. To one degree or another, we all experience insecurity. We doubt our abilities and our ranking in comparison to others (educationally, socially, financially, and so forth), and we even question whether or not God is really leading us. Due to our frailties, we are dealt a devastating blow whenever we have high expectations or imagine specific outcomes for ourselves but fall short of those expectations or performance goals.

THE TEMPTATION TO LEAVE OUR "BOAT"

When we experience these apparent failures, we second-guess our abilities, God's favor, and even whether the task we've devoted ourselves to is right for us. Yet I have found that God's next instruction for us often comes on the heels of our personal disappointments, failures, and unmet expectations. Let's look at a passage of Scripture that speaks to this issue.

> *One day as Jesus was standing by the Lake [or Sea] of Gennesaret, the people were crowding around him and listening to the word of God. He saw at the water's edge two boats, left there by the fishermen, who were washing their nets. He got into one of the boats, the one belonging to Simon [Peter], and asked him to put out a little from shore. Then he sat down and taught the people from the boat. When he had finished speaking, he said to Simon, "Put out into deep water, and let down the nets for a catch." Simon answered, "Master, we've worked hard all night and haven't caught anything. But because you say so, I will let down the nets." When they had done so, they caught such a large number of fish that their nets began to break. So they signaled their partners in the other boat to come and help them, and they came and filled both boats so full that they began to sink.*   (Luke 5:1–7)

Imagine the above passage as the beginning of a movie. It opens with Jesus observing two boats that were simply *"left"* at the shoreline. The camera then pans from the boats to capture a scene of pronounced discouragement as it focuses on several fishermen who had given up. They are holding cold, wet, empty nets in their hands as they wash them out with a look of discouragement and uncertainty on their faces.

These men had most likely started out the previous evening with eager anticipation concerning the possibilities of how many fish they would catch. They were competent and experienced fishermen who had been in the right place (water), at the right time (night and early morning), with the right tools (boats and nets), so they had every reason to believe their efforts would be fruitful and their endeavor would be a success. However, when they moved from theory into the water itself, nothing unfolded as they had planned. For hours, these optimistic fishermen had employed every skill and instrument in their arsenal—to no avail. Every time they threw out their nets and hauled them back onto the boat, there were no fish in them.

After ruling out their equipment as the problem, they may have begun to believe the difficulty was with the lake or their position on it. I'm sure they tried different locations and strategies, only to experience the same empty result. Perhaps it wasn't either of those issues. Maybe they thought, *Could it be that we've lost our touch as fishermen or are not as gifted as we thought?*

These are all possible scenarios for what had occurred during their night of fishing—the Scripture doesn't tell us specifically. However, it does say that they eventually pulled the plug on the job, went ashore, parked their boats, and began washing their nets to hang them up to dry after their failed endeavor.

Many people might dismiss their experience as just another day in the life of fishermen, but to do so would be to miss the symbolic illustrations and parallels for our own lives. This passage reveals not only the frustrations of a single workday for these fishermen but also a familiar season in the life of anyone who is used by God in His miraculous service.

While hosts of believers would have you believe that a walk with God is full of daily glory, I haven't found that theory to be based in reality. If we were completely transparent, we would have to admit that the valleys in our lives are just as real as the mountaintops, and that before clear answers arrive, there often come pronounced questions and deep uncertainty. While we may not be able to identify with washing and hanging up a literal net, I'm sure we can all identify with the symbolic parallel.

In the New Testament, nets can represent the ministry God has called us to—that which is more than simply an avenue of financial support but also brings spiritual fulfillment. We may not be literal fishermen, but the Bible tells us that we are called to *"fish for people"* (Luke 5:10). God has given all of us a unique "net," designed to be cast into the world in order to touch humanity and to draw individuals to Him. In addition to being given these nets, we have also been called to a specific God-ordained "sea," or unique context, for effective service. We're not all called to the same area or context of service; we have special settings where we'll excel the most. However, great frustration, disappointment, and even despair can set in when we've been laboring in our area with great expectations but little-to-no results. When you start with dreams of changing the world but can't see any progress in your dedicated endeavors, you can be tempted to come ashore and leave your boat.

For example, when the business you thought would both meet your family's needs and be a blessing to others is not providing money but instead consuming all your resources, you can be tempted to say, "Forget it!" and wash out your net. Likewise, if all of your education, preparation, and experience seems to offer you no advantages or measurable results, you may want to hang up your net, never to pick it up again. The disappointments of life are real and regularly tempt us not to believe, produce, or even try again. However, sometimes this is the very backdrop that the Lord wants speaks to us in. The question for us then becomes, "How will I respond to His voice at that moment?" Our answer to this question—and subsequent actions—will reveal our future effectiveness. Having the fortitude to respond to God's words, instruction, or commands in times of personal pain and discouragement is essential for anyone who desires to be greatly used by Him.

WHO RECEIVES THE GLORY?

Returning to the passage in Luke 5, we find a discouraged, dispirited Simon Peter who has worked tirelessly all night in hopes of a good catch, preparing to walk away from it all. Note that it is at that very moment that Jesus begins to speak to Him, saying, *"Put out into deep water, and let down the nets for a catch"* (Luke 5:4).

My question has always been, "Couldn't Jesus have intervened earlier?" Why allow the labor, pronounced disappointment, and wasted time before He decides to step in?" While I believe there are several answers that might be given in response to this question, one stands out to me more than the others. I believe Jesus waited—and still waits when it comes to intervening before disappointments or trials occur in our lives—because we often have difficulty making a distinction between results produced by our own efforts and those that come by God's mighty hand. Sometimes God will allow us to tire ourselves out or to become frustrated in our own efforts so that when He intervenes, there will be no doubt about where the credit belongs. While we may acknowledge to ourselves and even express the inadequacy of our efforts apart from God, there is a real difference between expressing this truth in theory and knowing it experientially. When we've come to the end of ourselves and depleted our desire, our strength, and our resource, and then the Lord turns everything around with a word, there is no question about who should receive the glory.

BEYOND HUMAN FRUSTRATION, LOGIC, AND FATIGUE

Somehow, even in his discouragement, Peter finds the resilience to respond to the voice of the Master. His willingness to obey in the midst of fatigue and disappointment, going against his own logic and experience, created the platform for Jesus to put His power on display through him. Peter could have very easily refused to follow Jesus' instructions based on his own past failures, lack of results, discouragement, or weariness. Basic reasoning might have been enough to deter him from making another attempt. After all, the carpenter-turned-religious-leader is telling the fisherman how to fish after Peter has used all of his own ingenuity!

Likewise, Jesus often speaks to us, too, when He finds us in such circumstances—jaded by past experiences, discouraged by a lack of results, or harboring anemic faith. Will we respond to God's word in the midst of our mental, physical, and emotional fatigue, and even against our own logic or experience, when necessary? Sometimes this is the environment that the Father requires us to respond in before we can experience His miraculous results. Peter responds to Jesus' command with the words, *"Master, we've worked hard all night and haven't caught anything. But because you say so, I will let down the nets"* (Luke 5:5).

While Peter does indicate the depth of his fatigue, he replies with respect and without a hint of cynicism. And he obeys the word of the Lord. While his experience had been frustrating, his faith in the Lord remained intact—and the events that followed have become the stuff of legends. Many believers have never experienced the results God wants to produce through them because they are willing to follow Him only up to the point of their frustration, and no farther. Others short-circuit God's display in their lives because they are willing to heed His voice only within the confines of human logic. Because Peter moved beyond his frustration and logic, he was able to experience something that was beyond human limitation. The Bible says that when he obeyed, *"they caught such a large number of fish that their nets began to break. So they signaled their partners in the other boat to come and help them, and they came and filled both boats so full that they began to sink"* (Luke 5:6–7).

SHARED BENEFITS

The last point to be made concerning our reaction to God in the midst of our frustration and seeming failure is that while our response is personal, the benefits we receive are shared. Peter responded in obedience to the voice of the Lord and was overwhelmed by the miraculous catch that followed. This catch, however, didn't fill only his boat but also the boat of his friends who were nearby.

I believe with all my heart that our obedient response to God's word is not only an opportunity for Him to reward our faithfulness but also a chance for Him to bless the lives of others through us. He is still the God who "opens up the windows of heaven and pours out blessing that we don't have room enough to receive" (see Malachi 3:10), but our abundance ought to benefit others. This truth should cause us to bounce back from failed and frustrating efforts and provide motivation for us as we journey through life's valleys. When we are discouraged, if we can't seem to find the fortitude to continue to follow the voice of God for our own benefit, we should do it for the sake of all those connected to us. Our families, our friends, our spiritual families, and our communities are waiting to receive the benefits of our obedience.

So pick up your net, push your boat back into the water, and let down your net again, this time believing that everything can be different—because you are doing so at His word.

A FINAL WORD

FLOURISHING BY GOD'S GRACE

There is no doubt in my mind that the miraculous life, and nothing less, is God's intent for His people—to see them flourishing by His grace in every area of life and relationship with Him and others. In no way is this life exclusively reserved for what is prominently miraculous; it can also be observed in the subtler interactions of life. Whether it's a sick body experiencing supernatural healing, an opening for a unique opportunity, divine clarity in a business meeting, or unusual wisdom that rests upon us while dialoguing with friends, we should live with the sense that we are functioning beyond our own human ability—often. In those moments, we should stop and savor the fact that we are not bound by the limitations of a strictly mortal existence but are, instead, in partnership with the God of infinite possibilities.

Our heavenly Father desires to receive glory for Himself by doing through us what we are helpless to do in our own ability. For this reason, we should make every effort to move into the type of reality He desires for us. Again, if you are not initially prompted to do this by personal desire, let it be for all those who will benefit from your obedience. If you are not motivated by the same cry that caused me to never want to live beneath the possibilities in Him, let it be done for His glory.

Like the prophetic voices and righteous reformers who have lived throughout the centuries, from Christ's first advent to this day, I, too, am consumed. Consumed with a desire for God's people to hear and respond to His divine utterances so that, as Jesus taught, "[His] *kingdom come*, [His] *will be done, on earth as it is in heaven*" (Matthew 6:10). It is our discernment of, agreement with, and obedience to His voice that unleash the immediate plans He desires to release, through us, to the world. This is exactly the pattern Jesus set for believers to follow Him into.

CULTIVATING RELATIONAL INTIMACY

With that in mind, a new concept of production and success should be embraced by every one of His followers. If our ultimate goal in this life is *"to be conformed to the image of his Son* [Christ]*"* (Romans 8:29), which is God's predestined plan for us, our conception of success should shift from the "How driven are you?" model to the "How well do you hear and respond?" model. Not that drivenness, disciplines, and methods aren't necessary, but we live in a time when these elements have been elevated prominently above divine utterance in the pursuit of success in ministry, business, and even domestic matters. While obedience to God's Word and His speaking can produce periods of increased drive, discipline, and methodology, we move closer to His conception of our success with every step we take toward alignment with His directives (both written and spoken). Jesus gave us a sense of a successful existence when He looked back over His well-executed ministry and life and declared to the heavenly Father, *"I have brought you glory on earth by finishing the work you gave me to do"* (John 17:4).

The declaration above allows us to observe that His success, in His words, was measured only by His obedient response to the heavenly Father's instruction through the execution of the work He gave Him to accomplish. Many who profess to be followers of Christ have not yet chosen to follow Him in this way of living. Rather, they have created models that gauge success based on targets God might not be concerned with and processes that are cleverly constructed but deaf to His present speaking in the person of the Holy Spirit.

Because Jesus followed the daily declarations of the Father from a place of cultivated relational intimacy, He did not have to wait until the end of His earthly life to feel a sense of fulfillment. He could rest His head nightly with a sense of purpose, accomplishment, and success, whether He had raised someone from the dead or had sat in discussion with His friends (disciples) for hours on end. This feeling of abundance came from the already established pleasure of His Father (which was granted before He ever performed one miraculous act) and the knowledge that He had responded to the Father's every word. While no one but Jesus has perfectly followed the will of God, there still remains a gem in the pattern He created. It is that the greatest fulfillment in life always comes from our obedient response to the Father. Therefore, our righteous response to God's heavenly utterances should not be just for the purpose of producing the miraculous but also to find fulfillment in obedience alone.

It is my heart's desire to see God's people arise with a consuming passion to pursue the life He has made accessible to them—a life of unusual possibilities, a life of transformative power, a life overflowing with fulfillment, purpose, and the God kind of success—the miraculous life.

OUR PRAYER

Father,

I thank You for the hunger that is building now in the hearts of Your people across this globe, an appetite that refuses to allow us to settle for anything short of a miraculous existence. I ask You to establish in our hearts a sense of the pleasure You take in bringing us into a deeper place of attachment to You and the delight that fills Your heart as we hear and respond to Your every word. I ask that as we, as Your people, do our part (hearing and responding), You will perform what only You can do (the miraculous). And we will attribute all the credit, glory, honor, and praise to You! Through the authority of Jesus the Christ, we pray and believe You will answer! Amen!

ABOUT THE AUTHOR

Wayne Chaney personifies the contemporary spiritual leader. He uniquely bridges people from different generations, cultures, and social demographics through his relevant teachings and spiritual insights. His rich family heritage of clergymen fuels his genuine love for people. He stewards a five-decade legacy left by his grandfather, Joe Chaney Jr., as he pastors Antioch Church of Long Beach, California. Wayne's determination to shift culture permeates his ministry expression, oratory, and brand.

Wayne has never been satisfied with the status quo, so whether it is through his national television show, radio broadcast, church congregation, regional festivals, or philanthropic work, he is destined to make a difference. Chaney is the visionary of the Long Beach Gospel Fest, one of the West Coast's premier gospel events held on the beautiful shores of downtown Long Beach. This yearly gathering brings politicians, business owners, gospel singers, and over twenty-five thousand people together for inspiration, worship, and music.

As cast members of the Oxygen Network's hit television series *Preachers of LA*, Chaney, his wife Myesha Chaney, and their three children shared their lives and family values with the world. Chaney has also appeared on *Extra, Access Hollywood, Showbiz Tonight, Arsenio Hall, The Real, Insider, Boris and Nicole, Lift Every Voice,* and *NewsOne Now.*

He is a featured radio talk show host on Stevie Wonder's KJLH 102.3 FM every Sunday. His weekly show *Real Life with Pastor Wayne and Myesha Chaney* has generated a considerable listenership because of its ability to tackle real-life issues and taboo subject matter with unique wisdom and grace.

Pastor Chaney has served on numerous local, national, and international boards, taskforces, and committees. These posts have ranged from grassroots organizations to some of the highest levels of national government. He has been the recipient of various awards, commendations, and recognitions and has also been featured in various publications, such as the *Los Angeles Times* and *Church Executive* magazine, for which he was the cover story. For two consecutive years, he has been listed as one of the *Long Beach Post's* "Ten Most Powerful People."

Pastor Chaney is happily married to Myesha and has three beautiful children, Wayne III, Reign, and Cadence.

Welcome to Our House!

We Have a Special Gift for You

It is our privilege and pleasure to share in your love of Christian books. We are committed to bringing you authors and books that feed, challenge, and enrich your faith.

To show our appreciation, we invite you to sign up to receive a specially selected **Reader Appreciation Gift**, with our compliments. Just go to the Web address at the bottom of this page.

God bless you as you seek a deeper walk with Him!

WE HAVE A GIFT FOR YOU. VISIT:

whpub.me/nonfictionthx

WHITAKER
HOUSE